"Tony Little is recognized around the country for his high energy approach to fitness. What good is an exercise program if you can't stick to it? Finally in TECHNIQUE!, Tony shows you what to do, and better yet, how to stay motivated."

—JOE WEIDER
Founder of *Muscle & Fitness* Magazine

"It's easier to exercise when you're inspired by the wonderful energy of Tony Little. He makes exercise fun and easy!"

—KIM ALEXIS, Supermodel

"Tony Little clearly is one of the most capable physical trainers in America today. His book will be a welcome addition to any fitness buff's bookshelf."

—DR. RONALD KLATZ, President,
American Academy of Anti-Aging Medicine
and Editor of *Longevity* Magazine

"Tony Little is an unbeatable combination of know-how and inspiration!"

—SUZANNE SOMERS

"TECHNIQUE! by Tony Little should be required reading for anyone interested in fitness. More than just talk, it's a step by step workbook to achieve your personal best. If you love fitness and don't have this book, you're trying to fish without a hook."

—BETTY WEIDER, Co-founder of *Shape* Magazine

"If you don't know how to exercise, do it with Tony Little!"

—VANNA WHITE,
America's Favorite T.V. Personality

"Tony Little's technique of combining low impact aerobics and specific resistance exercise to condition and reshape the body is the sagest and most effective system available. Add to this the intense motivation of Tony's one-on-one training and you'll make real progress on weight control, body rejuvenation and maintaining muscle tone."

—DR. WILLIAM A. LA TORRE, D.C., M.P.S.
Doctor of Chiropractic and Fellow, American
Academy of Biochemical Trauma

TECHNIQUE!

Target Training for a Fat-Free Body

Tony Little

with Paula Dranov

WARNER BOOKS

A Time Warner Company

A NOTE FROM THE PUBLISHER

The ideas, procedures, and suggestions contained in this book are not intended as a substitute for consulting with your physician. All matters regarding your health require medical supervision.

Copyright © 1994 by Tony Little Enterprises, Inc.
All rights reserved.

Warner Books, Inc., 1271 Avenue of the Americas, New York, NY 10020

Ⓦ A Time Warner Company

Printed in the United States of America
First Printing: November 1994
10 9 8 7 6 5 4 3 2 1

Library of Congress Cataloging-in-Publication Data

Little, Tony.
Technique! : target training for a fat-free body / Tony Little, with Paula Dranov.
p. cm.
ISBN 0-446-67072-3
1. Reducing exercises. I. Dranov, Paula. II. Title.
RA781.6.L54 1994
613.7′1—dc20 94-3439
CIP

Book design by Giorgetta Bell McRee
Cover design by Julia Kushnirsky
Cover photograph by Michael Grecco
Cover model Lee Ann Tweeden
Photos by John Clifford/Commercial Photographic Services

To all those who believed in me.

ACKNOWLEDGMENTS

Many thanks to . . .

The National Academy of Sports Medicine, Dr. Goldman and Dr. Klatz on assisting trainers

My Organization, Office, Partners, and Trainers

My Advisory Board

My family for support

Ray Manzella

Paula

The organizations who contributed charts and statistics

And, most of all to all my members, who believe in themselves first, then believe in me second to become part of their lives

CONTENTS

TECHNIQUE!

1
GETTING PERSONAL

tech·nique' (tek-nēk'), *n.* [Fr., from Gr. *technikos*, from *technē*, an art, artifice.]
    1. the method of procedure (with reference to practical or formal details) in rendering an artistic work or carrying out a scientific or mechanical operation.

Technique is the key to safe, fast and effective results.

If your car needed repairs, would you take it to the best mechanic in town or to a celebrity who collects cars?

If you needed an operation, would you go to the best surgeon you could find or an actor who plays a doctor on television?

If your son wanted to be a baseball player and you could afford it, wouldn't you hire the best professional coach you could find to train him?

Your body is your most precious possession—your vehicle throughout life. You can drive a Ferrari or a jalopy. The choice is yours alone. Are you going to trust it to some inexperienced celebrity or to a fitness expert—a certified personal trainer like me?

You want the best you can afford—the best mechanic for your car, the best doctor if you're sick, and a certified personal trainer with the knowledge, experience, and expertise to educate you, motivate you, and guarantee you results. You deserve it!

On this program you're going to redesign and redefine your body, change your attitude and your life. No matter what shape you're in today, you will be able to transform yourself more quickly than you ever imagined possible.

I'm going to give you the right input so you can get the right output. In the computer world, they speak of "garbage in, garbage out." It's the *programmer* who makes the difference.

In this book I'm your programmer and I promise you results.

You're going to change the actual composition of your body, trading ugly, useless fat for lean, shapely muscle without going on a starvation diet.

You're going to achieve super-high energy levels, too. The changes in your body will be reflected in your overall vitality and zest for life. A Ferrari isn't sluggish. It is sleek, fast, powerful and sexy—just as you will be as a result of this program.

2   With me as your one-on-one trainer, this program offers you a personalized workout, tailored to your body type, goals, capabilities and needs.

I know these are big promises, but on this program they will come true. I can guarantee you real and long-lasting results. My mission—my overriding passion—in life is to provide you with the right tools you need to achieve right results.

As an internationally recognized certified personal trainer and fitness specialist, I know what works and I absolutely know what doesn't. As someone who has suffered more than his share of physical injuries and mental obstacles on the road to success, I know what kind of exercise is both safe and effective and which workouts are a waste of your time, money, and energy.

> **One on one is the only way. It's personal, not general.**

This program works because it is scientifically based and easy to use. It has the approval of the National Academy of Sports Medicine, a professional organization of doctors who spend their lives treating injuries, advising athletes and making sure that the personal trainers they certify are up to speed on the latest and best advances in the *science* of exercise and weight loss.

WHY TECHNIQUE?

I have titled this book *Technique!* because it is the heart of my program. Technique is what makes any form of exercise effective. If you don't learn to work out the right way from day one, you might as well not work out at all. You won't get results, you may get hurt, and you most definitely will get discouraged. Safety is my number one consideration because it was an injury that changed my life and led me to develop this Total Body Rejuvenation program.

MY STORY

To begin at the very beginning of the commitment that led me to design this program, I would have to go back to a painful injury I received during a scrimmage in high school that disqualified me for the football team. I thought of myself as a jock, but with football now out of the question, I was a jock without a sport.

During my rehabilitation, I began to work out with weights. I really got into it and started to hang out at a local gym to watch the bodybuilders work. Soon I was hooked. I continued bodybuilding after high school and continued even when I became a salesman and was on the road all the time. All that travel didn't discourage me. I found gyms where I could work out, but more often than not there were none available, so I improvised. I believed then, as I do now, that there is always a way to make things happen. Working out made me feel good and positive about myself. I wasn't willing to sacrifice it just because I couldn't find a gym or the equipment I was used to in every area I visited.

In 1978 I won my first bodybuilding title, Mr. St. Petersburg (Florida). Over the next several years I did very well: I won the Mr. Suncoast title in 1979; Mr. Southern States in 1980, Mr. Southern USA and Mr. Florida in 1981, and, in 1983, Mr. Junior America.

By 1983 several national bodybuilding magazines had picked me as the favorite for the Mr. America title (now called the National Body Building Championships). I was training full-time, and I had my life mapped out. I would win the national title and then set my sights on the international competition for Mr. Universe. That prestigious

title would bring me the recognition that in turn would bring me product endorsements. I would then retire from competition, open bodybuilding clubs, and become a spokesman for the industry.

All those dreams went up in smoke on March 11, 1983, when a yellow schoolbus filled with elementary school children ran a red light and rammed into the side of my car with me in it and dragged me a full one hundred yards.

I saw the bus coming and knew what was going to happen, but I couldn't get out of the way. I was wearing my seat belt and just held on to the steering wheel with all my strength (which was a lot, considering that I was about to compete for a national bodybuilding championship). When the bus hit, my body was whipped sideways. Unbelievably, I felt no pain. At first all I could think of was the kids on the bus and whether they'd been hurt. I jumped out of the car and ran over to the bus to see if I could help, but the driver was freaked out and probably thought I was going to kill her. She wouldn't open the door.

By then I was surrounded by sympathetic and angry people who'd seen the accident and knew that the bus driver was clearly at fault. My adrenaline must have been soaring because the pain didn't hit until the police arrived. When they got me to the hospital, the doctors took one look at my huge neck and concluded that it was badly swollen and probably broken. I had to explain that I was a bodybuilder and that my neck always looked like that. By then the pain was overwhelming. My neck, my back, my whole body was screaming.

My neck wasn't broken, but I was in very bad shape. I had two herniated disks in my lower back and one in my neck. My knees were banged up, and my right shoulder was so bad that just holding a coffee cup in my right hand caused excruciating pain that brought tears to my eyes.

Incredibly, my sponsors insisted that I continue to train for the Mr. America competition. They had invested a lot of money in me over the years, and they convinced the doctors to put me on muscle relaxants and painkillers and forced me to compete. I didn't win. I came in fifth. (Eventually I repaid my sponsors' investment out of the damages awarded me for my injuries. Paying them back was a point of pride for me, but it left me broke and with no career.)

I spent the next two years in and out of hospitals. I was determined to avoid surgery, but the pain in my back was unbearable and nothing seemed to help. I began to gain weight and eventually put on more than fifty pounds. I was horribly depressed. My bodybuilding career was at an end. I was in terrible shape and had no plans for the future and no desire to make plans. To make matters worse, all of my friends from my championship bodybuilding days disappeared. That was another crushing blow. The loneliness and the realization that I had had so many false friends worsened my depression. That picture of me on page 7 says it all. Day after day I sat in my apartment, thinking about how much I'd lost. I kept looking above and asking, "Why me?" I had worked so hard, met all the goals I'd set for myself. I had perfected my body and sacrificed so much to train. I believed I would succeed. I believed in myself. And as a result of someone else's carelessness, through no fault of my own, I was left with nothing but pain, a badly damaged body, and a shattered career.

For months at a time I sat staring through the curtains, never going anywhere. My only entertainment was television. In retrospect, that is what saved me. I would get really irritated by the exercise programs. Those were the days when everyone was doing high-impact aerobic dancing, and the TV instructors with great bodies in great-looking leotards were jumping all over the place. Nobody taught anybody anything. They would just open the show, smile, and say, "Let's do it, let's begin!" without a word about how to prepare and how to do things the right way.

What about the people at home? I wondered. I was the people at home at that point, and I knew that if I were to try one of those workouts, I would reinjure my back in a heartbeat. What if someone trying to exercise along at home was overweight? There were no suggestions for easing into the program or modifying it. What if someone watching had back problems? Most of the movements were really risky. I knew that jumping around could lead to injuries just from jolts to the body from landing on a hard floor without the "give" of specially sprung gym floors. The more I watched, the more angry I became. I was convinced that the instructors weren't interested in the normal person who wasn't in good shape to start with. All they cared about was showing off their own great bodies with no thought, no compassion, and no real dedication to helping the people watching the show. Even today you can turn on the television and find programs that are just as bad. Some are worse because they use expensive gym equipment that none of us have in our homes.

I knew I could do a better job. At least I believed with all my heart that I could.

Suddenly I had something that I really cared about. My annoyance at TV exercise shows had evolved into a driving passion to create something worthwhile. I believed in exercise. I knew what it could do for self-confidence and a positive attitude. I knew it made life better. After all, where had I come from? My "before" photograph says it all. Exercise had made me a champion bodybuilder. I had used it to help myself. Now I could use it to help others.

But first I had to get my body in shape and saturate my mind with everything there was to know about exercise, fitness, and nutrition. I started working out again, but this time in rehabilitation programs designed to strengthen my back, reshape my body, and burn off the weight I'd gained. I knew that inactivity, not food, was to blame for the way I looked.

I also studied to become a certified personal trainer. I'm now certified by five national organizations, including the National Academy of Sports Medicine, and I have my own hospital advisory board to make sure that my workouts will educate, motivate, and help, not hurt, the people I train.

I was excited by the challenge I had set for myself, but, unbelievably, I encountered crisis after crisis that tested my commitment. The first was a bout of spinal meningitis, a life-threatening viral disease. I found myself back in the hospital for two days, hooked on intravenous feeding (a horrible way to lose twenty pounds). I had barely recovered when I accidentally sat in a pool of acid and burned my derriere so badly that I landed in a burn center, lying on my stomach, for two weeks. No sooner had I recovered from that than I was kicked between the legs by a horse and was back in the hospital. This time I had to lie on my back for another two weeks.

No one could believe my bad luck. Every get-well card contained a copy of the inspirational poem "Footprints." But I believed in myself and in God and was able to overcome the setbacks to develop a fitness program that works. My first criterion was that it be safe for everyone, even people (like me) with bad backs. That meant it had to be right for everyone at every level of fitness. It had to be nonimpact, with no running, jumping, or aerobic dancing. All of those activities are very jarring on the joints and very bad for

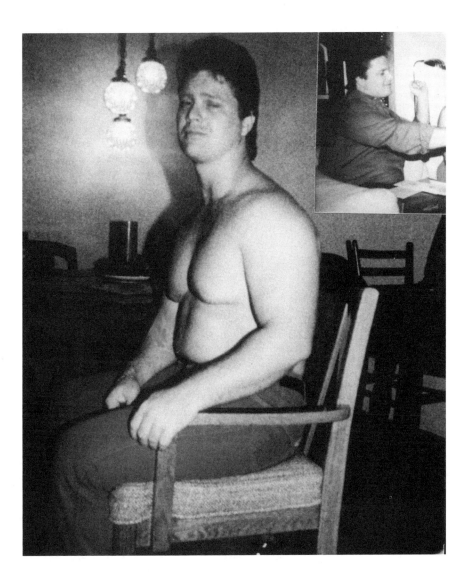

the back. I knew the same results could be achieved through nonimpact or low-impact exercise: walking, cross-country skiing, bicycling, and stair stepping on specially designed machines. But even those activities could be too strenuous for people who had been sedentary for years. I wanted to create a workout that would progressively build strength and energy, burn off fat, and reshape bodies. The program had to be safe, effective, challenging, fun, and adaptable enough to work for everyone regardless of sex, age, height, weight, or work schedules.

To do all that, a program must include all of the components of total fitness and fat loss:

- Strength training and muscular endurance for musculoskeletal fitness
- Flexibility and cardiovascular endurance for energy fitness
- Body composition (achieving a healthy ratio of muscle to fat) for nutritional fitness

8   After I understood exercise technique well enough to design an effective, balanced program, I went to my local cable station and pitched my idea for a show. They were interested but told me I'd have to cover the production costs. By then I was so committed to what I was doing and so passionate about helping people that I agreed to provide the money to produce the show.

Of course, I didn't have any money. But I did have an idea. That same day I created a company called TNT Cleaning, which specialized in cleaning health clubs, and I went right out and sold $60,000 in cleaning contracts. It was an incredible day: I started two new businesses, a television show and a cleaning company.

The show was a blockbuster success because it educated people about technique with humor, and provided fast results.

Two years later I wanted to make an exercise video. I needed investors to put up $100,000, but nobody knew me. I wasn't a national celebrity. I decided to ask one hundred people on the theory that at least three or four would consider helping me. One who agreed was the attorney who handled my lawsuit seeking damages from the automobile accident. He had watched me as I emerged from total defeat and began to believe in myself again. With his help I was able to produce my first video, *Bodycise*.

Then I had to sell it. I took it to a national video convention in Las Vegas, and I got offers from six major companies despite the fact that exercise videos featuring men had never been big sellers (95 percent of those on the market featured women). *Bodycise* was sold in video stores and was doing well, about two thousand copies a month. But that wasn't enough to get back the investment. I had to find an innovative way to sell more videos and let people know what a first-rate program I had developed.

I was convinced that the video would do well on the Home Shopping Network and went there to see if it could be sold on the air. The buyer turned me down. She said that for a product to be successful, it must generate a certain amount of dollars per minute, and videos had never sold well.

Later I met the son of Bud Lowell Paxton, the visionary who'd started the world's first shopping channel. Mr. Paxton's son owned a gym not far from my home, and we had a lot in common. He was able to get me a fifteen-minute appointment with his dad. Mr. Paxton told me essentially what his buyer had said earlier: videos had never sold well on the air. They didn't generate enough dollars per minute, and who was I, anyway?

But he decided to make me a bet. He said he would take five hundred videos and give them four different airings. If the videos sold out, he said we could do business in the future. *Bodycise* went on the air on a Saturday with a show host named Bobby Ray, who presented it the way I suggested with my "before" picture as a bodybuilder, a picture of me after the accident when I was overweight and depressed, and a picture of me after I got in shape.

All five hundred videos sold out in four minutes.

Mr. Paxton called to say it was hard to believe that the videos could sell out that quickly. He bought a thousand more, and they sold out in twelve minutes.

Then he asked me how I felt about going on the air live with a show host to talk to viewers about what I was offering, how it can help them, the benefits of nonimpact exercise, and my exercise beliefs.

We sold thirty-five hundred videos in fifteen minutes. I was a hit, and I've been with Home Shopping Network ever since.

My next move was into exercise equipment. At the time, the stuff on the market was

cheap, junky, and gimmicky. Celebrities were endorsing products that were no good. What's more, no one showed you how to use it or motivated you to work out. I decided to find the best home exercise equipment available (or design it myself to be sure it was safe, stable, and effective) and sell it with a personal training video in which I would explain each function, hop on the machine to demonstrate it, and work the machine myself at three different levels. I believe my line of exercise equipment has been successful because you get me as well as the machine. People who knew me from my videos and television appearances knew that I cared and had checked out the equipment to make sure it was the best available at the price.

I also began to sell personal training videos through infomercials. The first video was on an *Amazing Discovery* show, and I called it *Target Training*. It broke all records for videos sold via television: four million copies. I believe it did well because people were looking to work with experts who could educate them about technique, motivate them to use the technique, and guarantee them results. The infomercial became number one throughout the world, and has aired in twenty-seven different countries.

Believe in yourself and everything else will follow!
There's magic in believing.

BRIAN KUBIAK

Brooklyn, New York

Before her husband, Brian, started exercising and paying attention to what he ate, Denise was worried about him—and with good reason. He weighed 395 pounds.

"He couldn't walk down the street without losing his breath," Denise wrote. "He was depressed and constantly tired, the perfect candidate for a heart attack."

Brian was so heavy that when he developed painful gallstones, doctors didn't want to operate.

Using my program, Brian underwent an incredible transformation. He lost 190 pounds in the ten months after he began exercising. His doctors were astounded at the change. Brian was able to have successful surgery for his gallstones, and his life has changed tremendously. He has a whole new wardrobe. For the first time in years he actually enjoys buying and wearing clothes.

"I'm now living with a healthy and happy man," says Denise. "His legs are like an athlete's. He's firm, has a flat stomach and a gorgeous physique."

Brian had tried all sorts of exercise programs and diets before he found mine. But he couldn't stick with any of them. "I needed determination, willpower, positive thinking, and help—that's what you gave me," he wrote. "I'm now firm, happy, energetic, and more important, I'm healthy. I'm living proof that your program works!"

I guarantee that if it worked for Brian Kubiak, it will work for you.

SUCCESS STORIES

Business is booming, but my greatest thrill has been hearing from people who have bought my tapes and my fitness equipment. Their letters are overwhelming, absolutely incredible. People write about how they had been ripped off and taken advantage of and misinformed in their earlier attempts to lose weight and shape up. The letters come from everywhere, from all kinds of people with different problems and different lives. It's amazing to hear what happened to them once they had the right tools to work with and the information and motivation to make their dreams come true. Some have lost incredible amounts of weight. Their husbands and wives have written to thank me for saving the lives of men and women whose health was jeopardized by their weight and sedentary lifestyles. Sometimes I read the letters and want to cry. These are people who believed in themselves and believed in me. They identified with my passion to help them, my compassion for them, and my outrage that so much about the fitness business has been about business and not about people who need help.

You'll find their success stories and their "before" and "after" pictures throughout this book. You'll be able to see for yourself the amazing changes they have achieved. They're all people like you, skeptical at first that this program is any better than any of the others out there and could really make a difference in their lives. But you can't argue with the results they got. These are people who gave my method a chance and succeeded beyond their wildest dreams. They changed their bodies, their attitudes, and their outlook on life. Some were pretty desperate and in pretty sad shape.

You'll read about men and women who weighed hundreds of pounds more than they should. Some of them decided to embark on this program because their doctors insisted that they lose weight. Some had high blood pressure and high cholesterol. Some were so disgusted with themselves that they had lost their zest for life and had no real hope of making a positive change in their bodies and their attitudes. You'll be amazed at how quickly they were able to shed excess fat, reshape their bodies, and improve their health.

If I were merely to make claims about the effectiveness of my Total Body Rejuvenation program, you probably would suspect that I was making it all up. But seeing is believing. Pictures don't lie. The people you'll be reading about don't lie. Their words will help you understand that this program is every bit as effective as I say it is. More important, you will begin to *believe* that it can work for you. And it will. You'll see that this is a realistic program that helps real people with real problems. And it delivers real results.

LAURIE LANGDON

Littleton, Colorado

$\mathbf{L}$ook at Laurie Langdon. She was a chubby kid, and as you can see, a chubby bride. Now she's a professional model and a great inspiration.

"When we were kids, I was always teased about being twenty pounds heavier than my identical twin. And in my twenties I was engaged for a while to a man who mentally abused me. I felt pretty worthless and turned to food for comfort. Soon I had gained thirty pounds."

On her thirtieth birthday Laurie decided the time had come to do something about the way she looked. It was tough to fit her workouts into her busy day—she has three little boys and also baby-sits for a little girl. Between all the laundry, cleaning, and twice daily vacuuming, Laurie didn't have much free time for her workout. She had to squeeze it into the kids' nap time.

Her progress has been fantastic. Within two months she lost eight inches and fifteen pounds. Now, at five feet seven inches, she's down to a svelte 113, and her measurements are almost where she wants them: 34-24-34. Doesn't she look great? She feels great, too.

"My self-image has never been better," Laurie reports. "Now modeling agencies are calling me! I can hardly believe it. Becoming a professional model has been my lifelong dream."

AMERICA'S PERSONAL TRAINER

How do you think celebrities stay in shape?

How do Olympic athletes reach their potential?

They sure don't depend on celebrity videos. Can you picture Madonna, Demi Moore, or Cher exercising in front of the TV in their living rooms to another celebrity's video? You know as well as I do that they're very serious about staying in shape. They have to be. It's their livelihood.

Body-conscious celebrities have gyms in their houses and pay big bucks to personal trainers who come by on a regular schedule for one-on-one training sessions.

If you have the money, you can go to a gym in your town and pay a trainer $40 to $100 per session to teach you what I'm going to teach you in this book. The trainer will show you the exercises, stand there while you work out, count your repetitions, and urge you on when you get tired.

A good trainer will motivate you by challenging you with more repetitions or heavier weight and may introduce you to a new type of exercise to keep you from getting bored.

I'm going to do all that for you in this book.

Not only am I going to tell you what exercises to do, I'm going to teach you *how* to do them and explain the muscle groups they work and the guiding principles that underlie your success with this program.

You may be curious to know what it takes to become a certified personal trainer. I had the practical experience that came with being a national bodybuilding champion as well as firsthand knowledge of what's required in inner resources and determination—in my case, from learning how to rehabilitate and motivate myself after my automobile accident. But I also had to add to my education through qualifying programs that teach anatomy, structural integrity, exercise physiology, kinesiology (the study of human movement), and the psychology of exercise and nutrition. And then, of course, I had to pass a qualifying exam.

A certified trainer is not just a good body and a pretty face. A good trainer knows exactly what to do to educate you first, provide you with the right tools to achieve your goals, and motivate you so that you get the results you want.

As your personal trainer, I've spent years developing and refining a system that works. Everything you'll do as part of this program has been approved for safety by my medical advisory board. This book is going to become your exercise bible. It contains everything you and your family will ever need to know about getting in shape and staying that way.

Passion, patience and persistence always work.

14   HOW TO USE THIS BOOK

I've designed this book to educate and motivate you. In the chapters ahead I will give you all the information and all the tools you'll need to reshape your body. I'll teach you *technique*, the proper way to exercise for maximum effect. I'll explain how your body works, how and why you put on the pounds you want to lose, and how to change your body composition through exercise. I'll also tell you how to make simple changes in the way you eat to help fat melt away and stay away.

I hope you'll see this book for exactly what it is: a complete source of information to educate and motivate you, to rejuvenate your body and your mind. Use it as a workbook, and think of it as your link with me, your personal trainer. It contains the formulas we would use together if I were in your home to determine exactly how to tailor this program to your individual needs. If I were in your house with you, I would keep track of your progress. Instead, I'm giving you all of the charts you need to do it yourself. (Make extra copies if you're using this book with your spouse or a friend.)

It's very important to keep detailed records of your workouts. You need to know from session to session how many repetitions of an exercise you did the last time. When you get strong enough to exercise with weights (this will happen sooner than you expect), you will need a record of how many pounds you're using in each of the exercises you do.

Also, keep a food diary. It will help you identify the trouble spots in your eating habits. By keeping track of what you eat, you'll reinforce healthy changes in your daily diet that will help you lose weight, keep it off, and maintain high energy levels permanently.

Record keeping is terrific motivation. When you can look back and see the progress you've made in a short time, you'll be encouraged to keep going and to challenge yourself with each workout.

This is your *personal* training plan.

Together we will use it to achieve your fitness and weight loss goals.

CONCEIVE, BELIEVE

If you've seen me on television or seen one of my exercise videos, you know how often I repeat Dr. Norman Vincent Peale's credo: "Conceive, believe, achieve." At this starting point in your Total Body Rejuvenation program, you are going to take the first step: conceive of the changes you can make in your life and think about your goals.

What kind of body do you want? Do you have a clear picture of how you want to look? Concentrate on it. Think about the way you want to look. Form a mental picture of the body of your dreams. Memorize that picture. It is your goal. See your new body in your mind every day.

Conceive it. Believe it.

With this program you'll achieve it.

CONCEIVE, BELIEVE, ACHIEVE

THERE'S ALWAYS A WAY!

Focus first on your short-term goals, the ones you can achieve within weeks. I guarantee that after one or two weeks you'll have more energy, feel stronger, and have a satisfying sense of accomplishment.

As you move through this program from day to day, set goals for yourself. Challenge yourself every time you work out: add one more repetition, one more minute. You will succeed faster and see results sooner than you expect.

Now it's time to learn more about this program and how it works.

Are you ready to achieve?

2
A BALANCED PROGRAM

*B*alance is the key to the success of my program, so it's a word you will see over and over throughout this book. The balanced approach to fitness and weight loss I've developed will help you transform your body and your life. Each segment of this program is designed to complement the others, helping you to build muscle and burn fat at a rate you probably don't believe is possible. But it is!

If you have tried to lose weight and get in shape before—and who hasn't?—you probably are pretty skeptical that this program will succeed when so many others you've tried have failed.

But within days of beginning this program you will feel your body and your attitude changing. You're going to feel tighter, firmer, and stronger, and your energy level is going to skyrocket. Within weeks you will begin to *see* the difference. Your clothes will be looser in all the right places, and where you now have flab you'll begin to see shapely, toned muscles.

Once you feel and see results, there is no turning back. Success is a powerful motivator. You will find yourself looking forward to your workout. As you get stronger you will want to challenge yourself, set new goals for yourself. You will feel more in charge of your body and your life, and you'll have new confidence that your success is assured.

18 THE PROGRAM

There are three elements to this program:

1. *Musculoskeletal fitness.* This will come through strength or resistance training to build your muscles and change the rate at which you burn calories.
2. *Energy fitness.* Aerobic/cardiovascular exercise will burn calories and condition your heart, blood vessels, and lungs. It will enhance the fitness of your cardiovascular (heart and blood vessels) and cardiorespiratory (heart and breathing) systems.
3. *Nutritional fitness.* A no-nonsense, *no-diet* approach to healthy eating habits.

Here's how the three parts of the program work together:

1. Through resistance training you will strengthen and tone your muscles. This will change the ratio of muscle to fat in your body. The more muscular you become, the stronger and *leaner* you'll be. And since muscle tissue is more active metabolically than fat, it burns calories at a higher rate *all day long*, not just when you're working out. Resistance training will also deliver the first visual results of your Total Body Rejuvenation program.
2. Aerobic exercise like walking, running, biking, and swimming is calorie-burning activity. Your body draws the energy (calories) it needs to fuel exercise from your fat stores. While you're exercising, your body burns calories faster than it does when you're at rest. And it will continue to use calories at an accelerated rate for hours afterward. Aerobic exercise also conditions the heart and lungs, reduces the risk of heart disease, promotes general fitness, and relieves stress and tension.
3. On this program you are not going to starve. All you're going to do is cut down on the amount of fat in your diet by substituting satisfying and appetizing low-fat foods like breads, pasta, fruits, and vegetables for fatty ones like ice cream, red meat, butter, and fried foods. Since foods that are high in fat are also high in calories, making this healthy change is bound to help you lose fat.

So, you see, the plan is pretty simple:

By exercising, you will burn calories and burn them faster and longer as you become more muscular and shapely. And by making a few simple changes in your diet, you'll be consuming fewer calories even though you won't necessarily be eating less food. You *definitely* will not be eating diet foods. That is my winning combination for weight loss, good health, and a dynamite body.

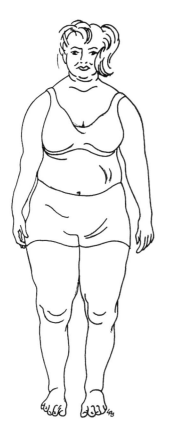
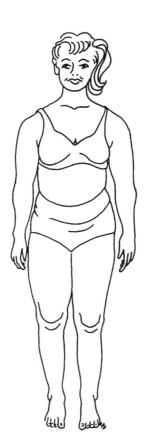
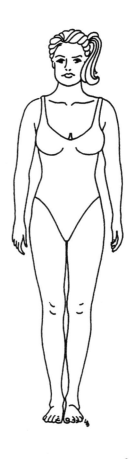

Before   *Diet without Exercise*   *Proper Eating and*
                                                    Exercise Balance

DREW SOUTER

Palm Bay, Florida

 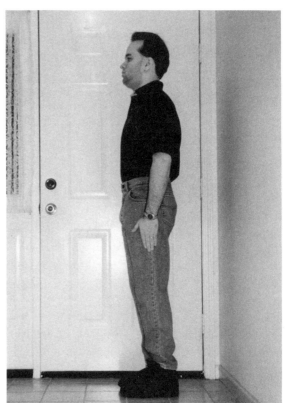

The story Drew Souter wrote me in December 1993 is a familiar one. Over the past six years he had become increasingly sedentary.

"I ate like there was no tomorrow and did little or no exercise. These bad habits coupled with my father's death in July of 1991 did me in. I gained fifty pounds and went from slim (165 pounds) to portly (215 pounds). My waist went from thirty-three inches to thirty-nine inches. I was twenty-seven years old and couldn't believe how bad I looked and felt. My blood pressure and cholesterol levels were higher than they should have been. Something had to be done and quickly!"

Drew began to watch what he ate and began looking for an exercise program but couldn't find one that made sense to him until he came upon mine.

By working out six days a week for four months, he brought the weight back down to 165 and his waist back to thirty-three inches. His blood pressure and cholesterol also returned to normal.

"Your program delivers results, results, results," Drew wrote. "I look and feel better than I ever have before."

This program is safe.

It is scientifically based.

It *always* works.

It worked for me. It worked for all of the people you'll be reading about in the pages ahead.

As your personal trainer, I guarantee that it will work for you, too, if you believe in yourself and believe in me.

TECHNIQUE

If you've seen me on television, you know how I carry on about technique. I can't overemphasize the importance of doing every single exercise in this book *exactly* as instructed. Frankly, I'm amazed that so little attention is paid to technique in other exercise programs. It is so basic to success that it's hard to understand why it's so often ignored.

Perfect exercise technique is the key to safe, effective, long-lasting results.

In fact, without correct technique you're wasting your time exercising.

Worse, you can hurt yourself. I don't know how many exercise-related injuries are due to poor or nonexistent technique, but I'm willing to bet that the number runs into the millions.

If your technique is wrong, you simply won't get the effects you want.

Think about it.

If you've ever played a sport, you know that correct technique is basic to success.

You can't hit a baseball without knowing how to hold the bat, and you can't hit the ball far without *perfect* technique.

You can't hit a tennis ball without knowing how to hold the racquet.

You can't hit a golf ball without knowing how to swing the club.

The same principle applies to exercise. To do it effectively, you have to know how to do it right!

In this book I'm going to tell you and show you how to do it right.

Proper Body Alignment
How to Be Strong, Flexible, and Focused

Proper body alignment is the foundation of technique. Once you learn proper body alignment you'll be ready for all the exercises in this book. You'll also find that you stand straighter and feel stronger, more flexible, more focused, and more sure of yourself whatever you're doing.

Proper body alignment makes every type of exercise easier and more effective. It "grounds" and stabilizes you so that you don't wobble and so that your movements are always as smooth, controlled, and effective as they should be. It also protects your back

22   from injury whether you're working with weights, doing your aerobic workout, or lying on the floor doing abdominal exercises.

    The pictures on these pages show a front, back, and side view of proper body alignment. Study them carefully. The idea is to align each of the major joints of your body over one another. You can see that the model's knees are aligned with her ankles, her hips with her knees, her shoulders with her hips. She looks stable and strong.

    From the bottom up, here's how to position yourself properly:

- Place your feet shoulder width apart with your toes pointing straight ahead. Make sure that your feet are flat on the floor.
- Flex your knees slightly and make sure they are positioned directly above your ankles.
- Tighten your thigh muscles.
- Pull in your abdominal muscles. If you don't keep them tight, your back is more vulnerable to injury.
- Lift your chest and pull your shoulders back so that your back is slightly retracted.
- Hold your head in neutral position, facing straight ahead. If you drop your head down or hold it up too high, you can injure your neck.

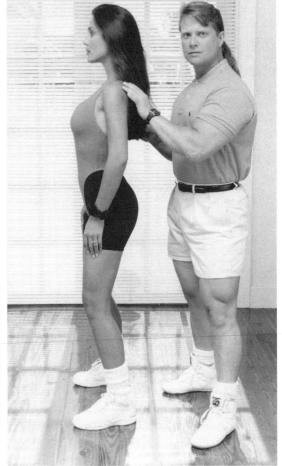

This is poor body alignment. I never want to see you standing like this!

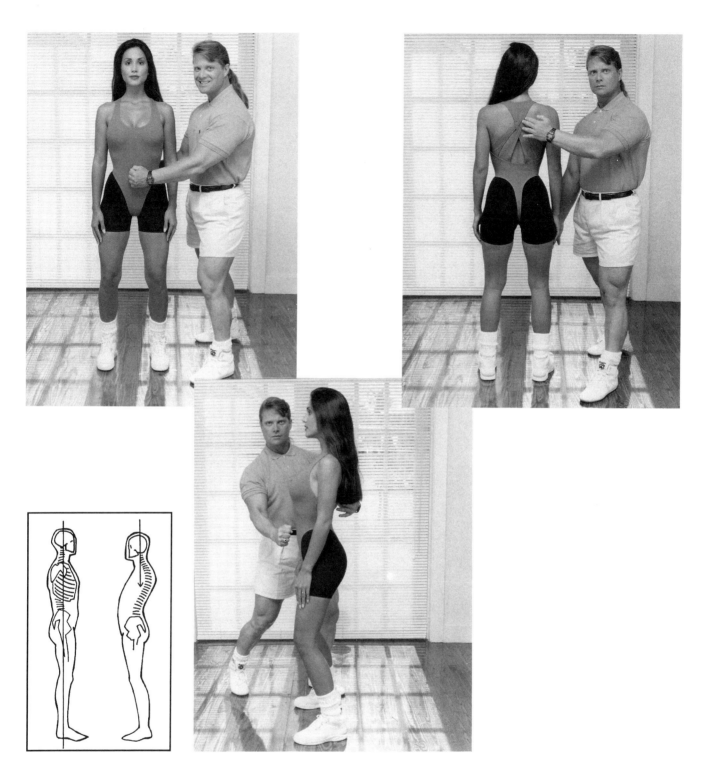

As your personal trainer, I'm going to remind you again and again throughout this book to check yourself for proper body alignment. If I were in the room while you are working out, I would be checking you, reminding you and repositioning you constantly. Proper body alignment before each exercise is essential if you want to achieve maximum results quickly and safely. In time, proper body alignment will become second nature. You won't even have to think about it when you begin to work out. And you will instantly feel the difference and know that something is wrong should your position change.

Proper body alignment is essential for fast, safe, amazing results.

FRAN DeSOURCEY

Mapleville, Rhode Island

I think you'll agree that Fran DeSourcey's story is truly amazing. From her "before" and "after" pictures you might think that she was in pretty good shape to start with, but the letter she wrote me early in 1994 explains how much she has changed:

"After my husband died two years ago, I felt as if I had died, too. I didn't care how I looked. I cried all the time. I couldn't seem to get enough sleep, and I wouldn't leave the house. I ate everything in sight, especially chocolate and cheesecakes. When I looked in the mirror, my reflection depressed me more. I was getting fatter and fatter, and I didn't even have the energy to put on a bit of makeup or comb my hair. Part of me wanted to die, but a tiny part of me was hoping for a miracle to change my life. I was being treated for depression, but the therapy didn't seem to help. I felt helpless and hopeless."

After hearing me tell my story on TV, Fran decided to order one of my exercise videos. At first she just watched the tape, but then she started exercising.

"Within a week I felt energy returning to my body and my depression seemed to be subsiding. I was feeling better just knowing I was doing something good for myself. Although I wasn't dieting, I lost ten pounds the first month and dropped from a size ten to a size five! I'm now almost fifty years old, and I look better than I ever did. Life is great, isn't it?"

RESISTANCE TRAINING

The first element of your workout is resistance or strength training. Over the next three weeks you're gradually going to begin working all the major muscle groups in your body. Slowly but surely you're going to strengthen and tone your muscles by working them against resistance. At first the resistance will come from your own body, but eventually you'll be using weights and adding more and more weight as you become stronger, more confident, and better and better looking.

Shape it.
Firm it.
Tone it.
Believe it!

The principles of resistance training are pretty straightforward and go all the way back to ancient Greece. Legend has it that the mythic strongman Milo of Crotana worked out every day by lifting a calf. As the animal gained weight, Milo got stronger and stronger. Supposedly he eventually hefted the full-grown heifer off the ground.

Today we can work out with weights and machines, not cows. But as far as strength training is concerned, not much has changed since Milo's day. I don't expect you to work with cows, calfs, or even light weights until you can easily do all of the exercises comfortably and *correctly* without weight.

Remember: The amount of weight you work with is secondary to technique. If you can't do an exercise with perfect technique, the weight you're working with is too heavy.

DON'T GET THE WRONG IDEA

Don't worry. Working out with weights on this program is not going to give you the bulging muscles of a bodybuilder. Women in particular often resist working out with weights because they think they'll get great big muscles. That simply can't happen on this program. In the first place, the weights you'll be using aren't heavy enough to build huge muscles. In the second place, this is a body-shaping, body-sculpting program, not a hardcore bodybuilding workout. When I was a bodybuilder I worked out for two and a half hours a day six days a week. Bodybuilding was the focus of my life. Believe me, you can't develop a bodybuilder's muscles by accident. But you can count on me to educate and motivate you so that you reach the goals you set for yourself in chapter 1 and achieve the body of your dreams.

26 MUSCLE DEFINITION

A lot of people are confused by the term *muscle definition*. They think it means big, obvious muscles. Well, it doesn't. Muscle definition is what you get when your muscles are strong and well toned and lend shape to your body. As you gain strength and lose fat, you will begin to see the shape of your body change. If you're just out of shape and not overweight, you will see this more quickly. If you're overweight, a new, taut body will emerge as the fat melts away. You'll look younger, more shapely, more fit and stronger. You'll see a curve in your upper arms, a squaring of your shoulders, a flattening of your abdominal area, a tightening of your thighs, and a nice, sexy V shape to your back. That's the way a healthy, beautifully toned body is supposed to look.

Can you imagine the way you're going to feel about yourself when you look like that? Can you imagine the energy you're going to have? With this one-on-one program and with me as your personal trainer, it will happen. Believe it!

Redesign and redefine your body, mind and dreams.

MUSCLE ISOLATION

In addition to perfect technique, resistance training requires concentration. You must think about the muscle you're working. Concentrate on it. You must *feel* the muscle working. Just going through the motions isn't enough. For example, if you're doing an exercise for your biceps and don't feel the work in your biceps, don't waste your time. Change something. Perhaps an alteration in your hand position will make the difference. Learn to be sensitive to your body. *Think* about what you're doing. You can't work out with your mind on "hold." If you pay attention to your body, you'll see results.

YOUR MUSCLES: MORE THAN 600 OF THEM

Yes, there really are more than 600 muscles in the body, and no, I'm not going to teach you exercises for all of them. Among your smallest muscles are the ones that control the movement of your eyeballs, the flaring of your nostrils, and the wrinkling of your forehead. The biggest muscle in your body is the **gluteus maximus**, your buttocks.

Forget eyeball-moving muscles. I'm going to put your butt and all your major muscle groups to work. You'll be concentrating on the big muscles that work your legs, power your arms and shoulders, hold you together in the middle, and determine the overall shape and contour of your body.

"Use it or lose it!" definitely applies to muscles. If you've ever seen what an arm or leg looks like after it has been immobilized in a cast for weeks, you have some idea of what happens when you don't use your muscles. Yuck. The body area involved looks shrunken and sickly. If you're a victim of the couch potato syndrome, your muscles have gotten slack, weak, and much smaller than they should be. When you don't use a muscle it doesn't just sit there on "hold," it shrinks. At the same time your percentage of fat cells go up and muscle cells go down. As a result, your metabolism slows, your energy levels drop, and you look and feel awful.

Luckily it's never too late to turn things around. Even geriatric patients in nursing homes have gained muscle strength via resistance exercise. If men and women in their eighties and nineties can do it, you can too.

And you must do it now. Life is too short to postpone the changes that will give you the energy you need to enjoy every day to the fullest.

A Muscle Primer

You will have a better idea of what you'll be doing on this program—and why—if you know something about the muscles you'll be working. The muscle map on page 28 shows you where the muscles are, and the paragraphs below explain the functions of all the muscles you'll be working on this program.

- *Abdominals:* Strictly speaking, there is only one abdominal muscle, the **rectus abdominis,** but we speak of the "abs" because the muscle is segmented to control the upper and lower areas of the abdomen. The rectus abdominis arises at the breastbone and ends at the pubic bone. You'll also be working the oblique muscles along the side of the abdominal wall. By strengthening your abdominal muscles, you can flatten and shape your midsection and better support your back. If your abdominal muscles are weak, your back is prone to injury and pain. Did you know that two-thirds of the strength for your back comes from the front, specifically your abdominal muscles? Some people hate abdominal exercises at first and find them difficult to learn. But once you can do them correctly, they're not hard at all. You'll be surprised at how much easier these exercises are when done properly. The secret is *technique.* And that is exactly what I'm going to teach you.
- *Thighs:* The **quadriceps** muscle ("quads") in the front of the thigh straightens the leg when you stand up. The muscle in the back of the thigh, the "hamstrings" or **biceps femoris,** move your hips and knees and rotate your leg. By strengthening these muscles, you can give your legs a sleek new shape. You will be toned to the bone and sexy or macho.

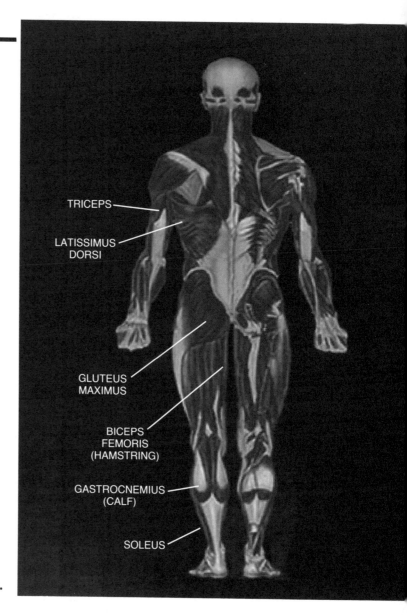

TRICEPS

LATISSIMUS
DORSI

GLUTEUS
MAXIMUS

BICEPS
FEMORIS
(HAMSTRING)

GASTROCNEMIUS
(CALF)

SOLEUS

Some of the basic,
larger muscle groups.

- *Buttocks:* The gluteus maximus, the largest muscle in the body, works when we stand up and when we climb. By strengthening this muscle, you can eliminate the "droopy buttock syndrome," a sure sign that you're out of shape. Strong buttock muscles also serve as a support system for your back. The stronger your buttock muscles are, the less trouble you'll have with your back.
- *Calves:* The **gastrocnemius** muscles in the backs of your lower legs work during walking and jumping. Just under the gastrocnemius is the **soleus** muscle, which works when you flex your foot. It also helps you stand. By strengthening both of these muscles, you can build up the back of your calves and get a beautiful, sexy heart shape. In my workout you're also going to exercise a muscle in the front of your lower leg, the **tibialis anterior**. Its normal job is to assist in walking, but if it's weak, it can contribute to ankle problems. By strengthening it, you can add a pretty new shape to the front of your lower leg. Legs! Legs! You will have gorgeous legs!
- *Chest:* The fanlike **pectoral** muscles in your chest work to move your arms. They hold up a woman's breasts and make a man look more masculine.

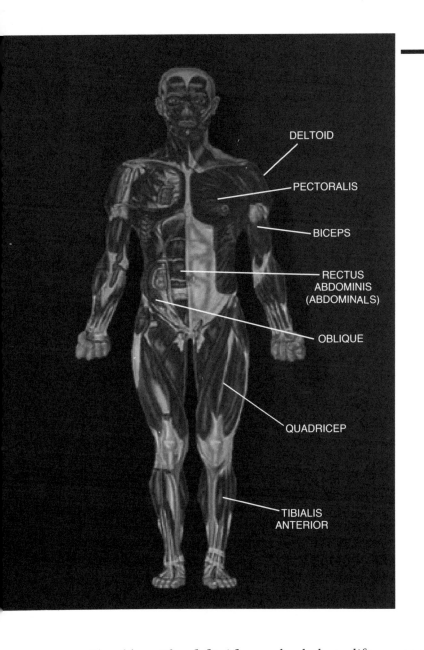

DELTOID

PECTORALIS

BICEPS

RECTUS
ABDOMINIS
(ABDOMINALS)

OBLIQUE

QUADRICEP

TIBIALIS
ANTERIOR

- *Shoulders:* The **deltoid** muscles help to lift your arms, give your shoulders shape, and enhance your upper body posture.
- *Back:* One of the major muscles in your back, the **latissimus dorsi** (lats), run from the middle of your back to your tailbone. They move your shoulders. Properly developed lats will give your back a sexy V shape and make your waist look small. They're not the only muscles in your back. You'll be working many others during this program, like the *trapezius*, which are in the upper back and hook into the shoulder.
- *Arms:* The **biceps** muscles in front of the upper arm rotates and bends your forearm. Although it looks like one muscle, it actually has two heads—that's why it's called the *bi*ceps (*bi* is from Latin, meaning "two"). Every guy likes great biceps.
- The **triceps** in the back of the upper arm is (you guessed!) a three-headed muscle. The triceps work to straighten the arm. Women must not use it enough in the normal course of events because their upper arms can get awfully flabby as the years go by. But you're going to get rid of those "granny arms." Wait and see. You will have toned, firm arms.

WORKING YOUR MUSCLES

The way to build, firm, and strengthen muscles is to challenge them progressively. You start off doing the exercises against the resistance of your own body. When the exercises are no longer challenging, you do more of them (more repetitions). Then you add weight (dumbbells). And when the weight is no longer challenging, you do more repetitions, and when your workout again becomes easy, you add more weight.

That's about all there is to it.

Weight training is done in series of repetitions ("reps") and sets.

Repetitions is the number of times you do a particular movement. **Set** is the sum total of the repetitions. You may do one or two sets of eight to ten repetitions each.

Since men and women usually have different goals, their strength or resistance training workouts will be slightly different.

Women usually want slim, shapely, well-toned bodies: tight butts, flat abdomen, and shapely thighs. They can get results by using light weights and doing more repetitions per set. For example, a woman might do two sets of fifteen repetitions each while a man who wants to build a strong physique would do two sets of eight with heavy weights. Men who want to build an athletic, strong physique must use heavy weights and do fewer repetitions per set.

Rules to Remember

1. The correct *technique* for picking up weights is to bend your knees, squat, and use your legs, arms, and upper body to lift them all at once. Don't just bend over and try to pull them up. You can (and most likely will) hurt your back even if the weights aren't particularly heavy.

2. The correct *technique* for working with weights is to concentrate on slow and controlled movement. Never jerk or swing the weights. If you can't maintain proper technique, the weight you're using is too heavy for you. *Never* sacrifice control (technique) for heavier weight. If you do, you'll end up with joint pain and no results instead of great results, high energy, and renewed self-confidence.

3. Increase the amount of weight you're using only when your workout is no longer challenging at the number of repetitions and sets you've been doing and with the amount of weight you had been using. And then increase only in small increments.

TAKING YOUR MEASUREMENTS

Before you start this program, record your measurements on the chart below. You're going to see some amazing changes in your body, and I want you to have an accurate record of your progress "before" to "after." Make a note of your measurements in the space provided. Don't cheat and pull the tape measure tight. Round off each measurement to the nearest half inch.

TONY LITTLE'S INCH REDUCTION CHART

Use the chart below to log your changing measurements. Every four weeks use a tape measure to determine your measurements at all of the body sites indicated.

Remember: Do not use a weight scale. It is your worst enemy because it measures fat, water, and muscle loss or gain, not just fat. Because muscle weighs more than fat, and because water makes up most of your body weight and fluctuates daily, a scale tells you very little about fat loss and lean muscle gain.

As you continue using my Total Body Rejuvenation program, you will notice a slimmer, more shapely you.

Measuring Sites:

| *Neck* | *Arm (L/R)* | *Hips* | *Calf (L/R)* |
| *Bust/Chest* | *Waist* | *Thigh (L/R)* | |

Measured in Inches	Week #1	Week #4	Week #8	Week #12	Week #16
Neck					
Arm—Right					
Arm—Left					
Bust/Chest					
Waist					
Hips					
Thigh—Right					
Thigh—Left					
Calf—Right					
Calf—Left					

32   THROW AWAY YOUR SCALE!

You may be wondering why I didn't ask you to record your weight along with your measurements. I don't care what you weigh, and neither should you. As a matter of fact, I don't want you to weigh yourself regularly while you're on this program. Nothing can be more discouraging. Your weight is the sum total of the bones, fat, muscle, and water in your body. Whatever your size, water makes up 65 percent of your weight. The numbers on the scale tell you very little about fat loss or how the ratio of lean muscle to fat is changing in your favor over the course of this program.

I know that regardless of what I tell you, you will probably check the scale from time to time. But please don't weigh yourself every day. The changes you see reflect fluctuations in water balance. At certain times of the month women retain water easily. This can show up on the scale as a weight gain, but it means *nothing* in terms of muscle to fat ratio. If you're sensitive to salt, you can see a big weight gain on the scale the day after eating Chinese food. The salt traps water in your body, and the gain reflected on the scale is just water and will disappear after your system flushes out the excess fluid in a day or two.

All told, what your scale tells you can be very depressing and misleading. Ignore it.

On this program, changes in your measurements, the way your clothes fit, and the way your body feels are much better, more long-lasting indications of your progress.

THE IDEAL WEIGHT MYTH

I also want you to forget about the concept of "ideal weight" while you are on this program. Weight matters only when the excess reflects too much fat, not too much muscle. And believe me, you can be at your "ideal weight," look thin, and still be too fat. Do you know anybody who looks great in clothes but terrible in a bathing suit? The clothes hide a body that is slack and shapeless, the result of too much fat and too little muscle. I'm sure you can see the difference between a 250-pound football player who is all muscle and a 250-pound couch potato who is too fat. Both men may be the same height, but their bodies will bear no resemblance to each other. One will be firm, hard, well muscled, self-confident, and energetic. The other will be spongy, flabby, fat, lethargic, and self-conscious about the way he looks.

METABOLISM

Strictly speaking, metabolism is the process by which our bodies create and consume energy. The vast majority of daily calories fuel the body's basic physiological functions

Who wants to carry around all that ugly excess fat? Look what 20 lbs. can do to your posture!

like breathing, circulation, cell building, and digestion. This "bottom line" of energy consumption is called the **basal** or **resting metabolic rate.** The more active and the more muscular you are, the more calories you burn beyond your basal metabolic rate.

Active body tissue like muscle burns more calories than inactive tissue. Fat is about the most inactive and ugliest tissue there is. It just sits there. It's energy waiting to be spent, and the reason it accumulates is that it isn't being used up fast enough.

The rate at which you burn calories is determined by how active you are and your body's ratio of lean muscle tissue to fat. Increase the amount of lean muscle tissue and you will burn calories faster and feel more energetic. Let muscle tissue atrophy through disuse and you will burn calories slower—and get fatter and more sluggish.

You can use the spaces below to figure your basal or resting metabolic rate. Just multiply your weight by 11. If you're inactive, add another four hundred calories, the amount needed to fuel sedentary activities like walking to your car, driving, and moving about during the day.

Your weight: _____ × 11 = _____ (BMR)

34   THE PERFECT BODY

Ideally, no more than 18 percent of a man's body composition should consist of fat. For athletes fat may make up a very low percentage of total body weight. When I was a bodybuilder my body fat was down to only 6 percent. Women need a bit more body fat than men—between 20 and 25 percent to keep their hormonal systems functioning normally. When a woman's body fat falls too low, she'll stop producing adequate amounts of the female hormone estrogen. She will no longer menstruate and won't be able to get pregnant. And since estrogen is also needed for normal bone building, a woman who no longer menstruates because her fat stores fall too low can actually begin to lose bone, even at a very young age.

HOW FAT ARE YOU?

For an *exact* measurement you have to get weighed underwater, a complicated and expensive procedure used only in sophisticated research laboratories. However, you can get an approximation of your muscle to body fat ratio with calipers, a device to pinch and measure flesh at four spots on your body. (Instructions on measuring body fat with calipers are in appendix 1.)

You can also use a mathematical formula called the Quetlet index to get an approximation of how much of your weight is fat. Although the formula is relatively accurate for normal, sedentary people, it isn't exact, and will overstate body fat for athletes, bodybuilders, and anyone else who is very muscular.

The calculations aren't difficult, but there are a few steps. Use a calculator and write down the result of each step. First you have to translate your weight into kilograms and

QUETLET INDEX CALCULATION OF BODY FAT PERCENTAGE

FORMULA	EXAMPLE
1. Translate your weight into kilograms (divide by 2.2).	160 ÷ 2.2 = 72.7
2. Translate your height into meters (multiply your height in inches by 2.54 and divide by 100).	5 feet 4 inches = 64 inches 64 × 2.54 = 162.56 162.5 ÷ 100 = 1.62
3. Figure the square of your height (multiply it by itself).	1.62 × 1.62 = 2.6
4. Divide your weight in kilograms by the result of step 3.	72.7 ÷ 2.6 = 27.9

your height into meters. Here's the step-by-step guide using a five-foot-four, 160-pound woman as an example:

The woman I used for the example has a body fat percentage of about 28 percent—a bit too high for the 20 to 25 percent range recommended for women.

Use the spaces provided below to calculate your own body fat percentage.

1. Your weight _____ divided by 2.2 = _____
2. Your height in inches _____ × 2.54 = _____
3. Now, divide the result of step 2 by 100: _____ – 1— = _____
4. Multiply the result of step 3 by itself: _____ × _____ = _____%
5. Divide your weight in kilograms by the result of step 4: _____ – _____ = _____

NO EXCUSES

Do you know the number one excuse people give for not exercising?

They don't have time.

If I have time, you have time.

Do you know when I do my workout?

At 4:30 A.M.

Okay, so I'm a little unusual.

The truth is, my days have become so hectic that if I don't get up extra early to exercise, I would never get around to it. And I wouldn't have the energy and strength to handle my crazy schedule with enthusiasm.

And who ever heard of a personal trainer who doesn't work out?

The first week of this program requires only fifteen minutes a day. I know you can spare fifteen minutes out of twenty-four hours.

The second week you will need an extra fifteen or twenty minutes three times a week.

During the third and fourth weeks your workout will take thirty minutes a day or less, six days a week.

By then you'll notice a difference in the way your body feels. You may see a difference in the way you look. Your attitude will improve, too. Once you see results, you won't be worrying about time anymore.

The Best Time to Work Out

People always ask me *when* to work out. Is the morning best? The evening?

The time of day doesn't matter. You have to find a time that is right for you. If you're an early riser like me and don't mind getting up a little earlier, do your workout first thing in the morning. It's great to start the day already having done something good for yourself. And you won't have to think about working out again until the next morning.

But there's nothing wrong with working out later in the day. If you can get home or get to a gym during your lunch hour, do your workout then. Or do it after work and before dinner. As long as exercise becomes part of your daily routine the time of day isn't important.

It isn't a good idea to work out on a full stomach. You probably won't be comfortable. Schedule your workout before meals or at least two hours after eating.

BREATHING

All forms of exercise are easier and more effective if you breathe properly while working out. Try to exhale through your mouth on the exertion and inhale through your nose when you relax.

As helpful as correct breathing is, at first it's more important to concentrate on technique and learn how to do the exercises correctly. I'll remind you about breathing as I describe the exercises in the chapters ahead.

However, don't hold your breath while you exercise. If you do, you'll find yourself winded and tired. Just breathe normally. If you find that you're holding your breath, try to break the habit by exhaling on the exertion. You will inhale automatically.

SIXTEEN WEEKS TO A DYNAMITE BODY

Whatever shape you're in today, you're going to see a major improvement over the next sixteen weeks. That doesn't mean that you can stop exercising at the end of sixteen weeks. To stay in shape you have to continue. But in sixteen weeks you will be so happy with the way you look and feel that, believe me, you wouldn't dream of giving up this program. Your new, streamlined body—your elite physique—will be all the motivation you'll need.

Week One: Your Total Body Rejuvenation program begins in chapter 3. You'll be concentrating on your abdominal and back muscles. Your total time commitment will be about fifteen minutes a day, Monday through Friday.

Week Two: During the second week you will continue with abdominal and back exercises every day but add six exercises for your lower body (buttocks, hips, and legs), to be done three times a week, on Monday, Wednesday, and Friday or on Tuesday, Thursday, and Saturday.

Week Three: Alternate exercises for the upper body (chest, shoulders, and arms) with the lower body workout. You now will be exercising six days a week. You'll do your abdominal exercises every day, lower body exercises on Monday, Wednesday, and Friday, and upper body exercises on Tuesday, Thursday, and Saturday.

Week Four: Now you add aerobic exercises for calorie-burning, cardiovascular, and cardiorespiratory fitness. You'll do an aerobic workout every other day, and upper and lower body and abdominal workouts on the alternating days. You'll be working out six days a week.

Weeks Five through Eight: Continue alternating aerobic and resistance training workouts. You can now increase repetitions and weight. For variety and challenge you will do a different type of aerobic/cardiovascular exercise from the one you chose in week four.

Weeks Nine through Sixteen: Instead of doing your resistance training on one day and your aerobic workout on another, you'll do aerobics every day and alternate your upper and lower body workouts. During these weeks you will take every fourth day off. You'll also be increasing the amount of weight you're using and the length of your aerobic workout.

WORKOUT FUNDAMENTALS

Every workout begins with a warm-up and stretching and ends with a cooldown.

For safety's sake, never, never skip any of these essential elements.

A warm-up simply means moving your body for three to five minutes before you begin to exert any effort. The movement "warms" your body by bringing blood to the muscles that will be used. The warmer muscles are, the more flexible and less prone to injury they'll be. Warming up also helps avoid cramping by preventing blood from pooling.

No athlete goes into competition without a warm-up. Think about pitchers in the bullpen. Think about tennis players volleying before a match. They know the value of properly preparing their bodies for exertion and the price of neglecting to warm up. If you fail to warm up, you can hurt yourself. The injury will prevent you from working out. As a result, you'll stay fatter longer.

Stretching is essential, too. And by stretching I mean *static* stretching, a term that may be new to you. A static stretch is slow and controlled. *Never* bounce. Stretch only as far as you comfortably can. You want to feel the stretch in your muscles, but you don't want to hurt yourself. Throughout this book I'll be describing specific stretches for specific workouts. Do them religiously. If you don't, you'll be sorry.

Cooling down after a workout may be as simple as stretching the muscles you've used or just slowing your movements until your heart rate returns to normal. The cooldown helps your body recover from exertion and avoid injury. Cooling down is especially important after an aerobic workout, when your heart has been beating much faster than it normally does. Ending an aerobic workout without a cooldown is like slamming on the brakes in a car going seventy miles an hour—you'll be very uncomfortable. You could get dizzy and faint. You could even have a heart attack. And die.

Have I made myself clear?

Now get ready for your first workout.

I want you to get active and enjoy life. You can do it!

3
Week One:
ABDOMINAL WORKOUT

The first week of your Total Body Rejuvenation program will concentrate on stretching and resistance exercises for your abdominal and back muscles. Throughout the program I'll emphasize protecting your back and preventing back injuries. I've had so many problems with my own back that I'm supersensitive on the subject. Besides, back pain is surprisingly common: sooner or later more than 80 percent of us develop problems. If your back has ever bothered you at all, you'll be glad to know that you can do these exercises safely if you follow my instructions to the letter. Technique is the key to safety and effectiveness. You can easily injure your back if you do these—or any other—exercises incorrectly. And if you do them right, they'll strengthen the muscles that support your back and help you guard against future problems.

You may be wondering why abdominal exercises are good for your back. Remember: Two-thirds of the support for your back comes from your front, specifically your abdominal muscles.

Of course, your back isn't the only consideration here. How about midriff bulge? Those love handles? (In Canada they call them "Molson muscles" in tribute to the country's popular beer.) That gut? Abdominal exercises are going to help you tone, firm, and strengthen the muscles so that your midsection will look lean and tight.

If you've done abdominal exercises in the past, you probably will be surprised by the ones you'll be doing this week. There isn't a sit-up in sight ... because sit-ups don't work. Instead you'll be doing abdominal curls that concentrate the effort only on the muscles you are trying to affect. Once you learn the proper technique, you'll be amazed at how easy and effective these exercises are.

During week one of your workout program, you're going to exercise your abdominal and back muscles Monday through Friday. That's right: five days. Regardless of your exercise experience, I want you to begin this program at the beginner level. You can move on to the intermediate level as soon as you master exercise technique and the beginner level becomes easy for you.

REMINDER: *Never* begin this program at the advanced level even if you have lots of exercise experience. "Advanced" is only for those who have perfected exercise technique and find the intermediate level too easy. Since you haven't learned my program yet, you haven't mastered technique!

GETTING READY

You'll need the following equipment for your abdominal workout:

- An exercise mat. If you don't have one or don't want to invest in one now, pile two or three small scatter rugs on top of each other and cover them with a bath towel. Your work surface should be well padded, with some "give." Test it out to be sure you'll be comfortable lying on your back.
- Your workout gear. Tights and a leotard are fine for women, and cotton-spandex biking shorts and a T-shirt will work for men. (If you don't have tights or biking shorts, just wear loose-fitting clothing that allows you to move easily.) Wear athletic shoes. Never work out in bare feet or in street shoes or slippers. You need the stability and support only comfortable, lace-up athletic shoes provide. I recommend cross-training shoes.

WARMING UP: Before exercising, it's important to get the blood flowing and loosen up your muscles. So move that body to some music for five minutes. Don't push, just mobilize.

STRETCHING

Begin your workout with the stretches described below. They'll help prepare your muscles for exercise.
Hold each stretch for ten counts.

- *Low back and hamstring stretch* (for the erector spinae and hamstring muscles in the lower back and the back of the legs): Slowly lower yourself to the floor and lie down on your back, bending your knees. Gently hug your knees into your chest as shown in picture B. Be sure your hands are under, not over, your knees.
- *Alternate low back stretch* (for the erector spinae and hamstring muscles in your lower back and the backs of the legs): Lying on your back, bend your left knee and place your left foot on the floor. Raise your left leg up into the air as shown in picture D. Your knee should be flexed slightly. Gently pull your leg toward your chest. Repeat for the right leg.

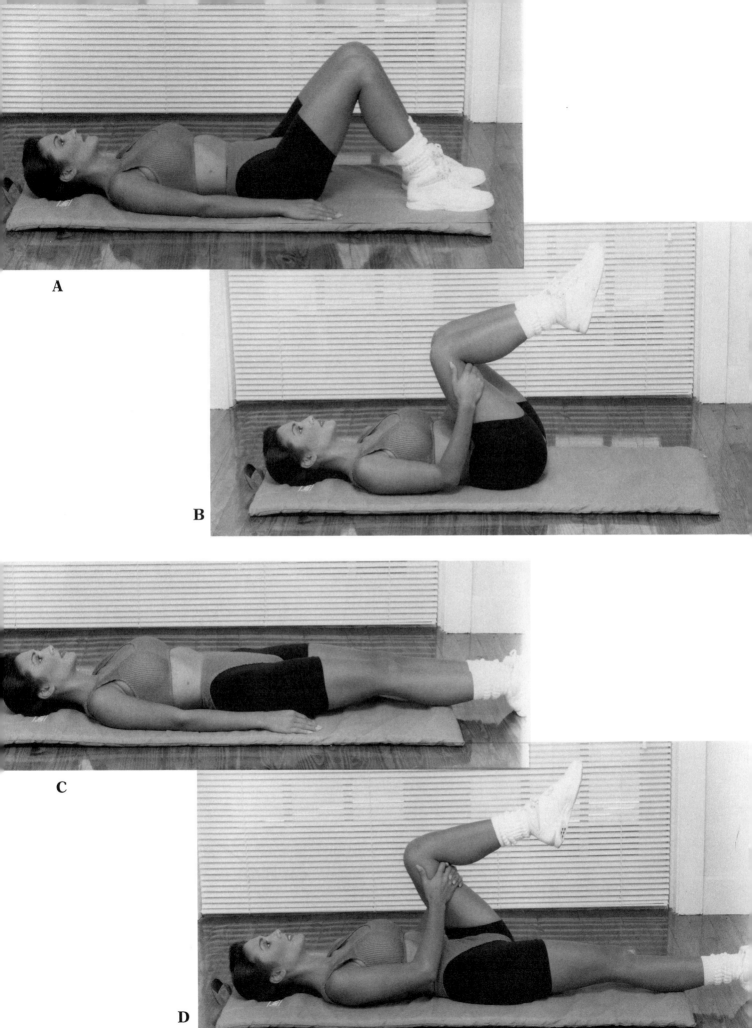

A

B

C

D

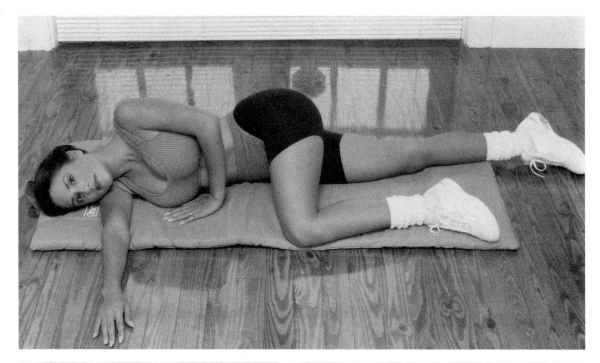

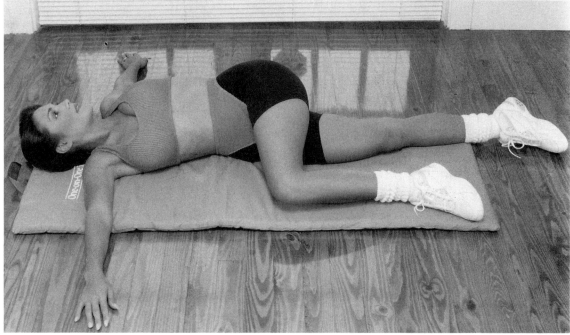

- *Lateral low back stretch* (for the erector spinae, abdominal, and oblique muscles in your shoulders, upper body, and midsection): Lying on your right side, bend your left leg at the knee and stretch it toward the floor as shown above. At the same time, stretch your left arm in the opposite direction as far as you can. As you become more flexible, you'll be able to stretch your arm farther. Repeat lying on your left side.

- *Full back and hip stretch* (for the latissimus dorsi and other back muscles, gluteus medius, gluteus maximus, and quadriceps muscles in your back, hips, buttocks, and legs): Sit back on or between your heels and stretch your chest and arms out on the floor in front of you as shown above. Stretch only as far as you comfortably can.

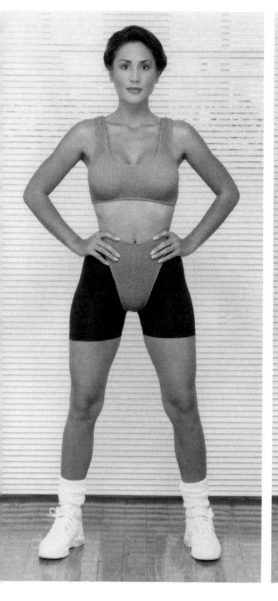  

- *Lateral neck stretches* (for the trapezius muscles in the side of your neck): While standing in proper body alignment, stretch your head to the right as if you were trying to touch your ear to your shoulder, as shown above. Do this gently. Never force this stretch. Repeat for the left side.

- *Frontal and posterior neck stretch* (for the trapezius muscles in your neck): Stretch your neck by raising your chin. Then bend your head toward the floor as shown above.

Now you're ready for your workout. Never forget to do an active warm-up and stretching beforehand.

THE WORKOUT

The difference among the beginner, intermediate, and advanced levels is the number of repetitions (reps) you will do. This week I want you to concentrate solely on technique. It's the key to fast, safe, effective results. Once you're confident of your technique, you can move on to the next level as soon as the workout becomes easy.

- *Beginner:* six to eight reps
- *Intermediate:* ten to fifteen reps
- *Advanced:* sixteen to twenty-five reps

BREATHING: Remember to breathe normally as you exercise. Don't hold your breath.

Exercise #1
●
ABDOMINAL CURLS

This exercise is going to tone and strengthen the rectus abdominus muscles in your midsection. Picture A shows the proper position.

- Lie down on your back. Make sure your back is flush to the floor.

- Bend your knees and place your feet flat on the floor at about the width of your shoulders.

- Place your hands on your stomach so that you can feel the movement. If you've had any neck problems or if your neck starts to hurt while you're exercising, support your head lightly by placing your hands on your head just above your ears or fold your hands together as if you were praying and put them under your chin for extra support.

A

B

- Now, *squeeze* your abdominal muscles as hard as you can. Aim them toward your spine. You should be able to see your abdomen pull in.

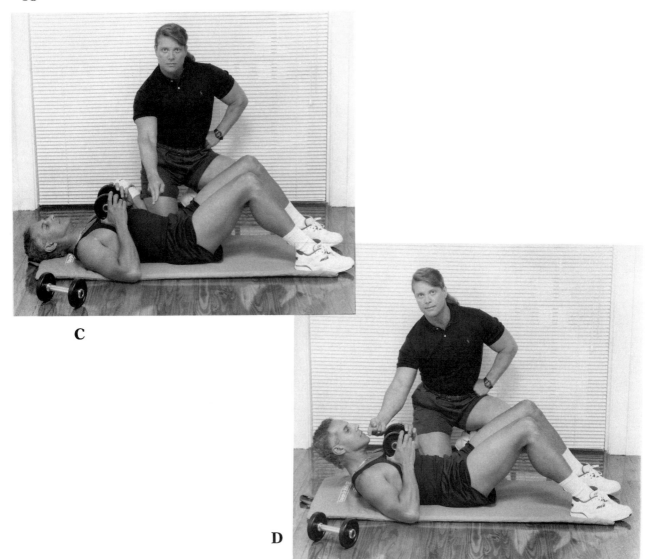

C

D

- Raise your upper body and squeeze as shown picture C. As you come up, exhale through your mouth. Don't push for height or reach for your knees. This movement is small and concentrated. It's *not* a sit-up. It's a very small movement. The picture shows what you are aiming for. Be careful not to jerk yourself up. The curl should be smooth and controlled. Eventually you'll be able to work out with weight, so the picture shows how the move would be executed. But don't even think about weights until the advanced level becomes easy.

- Hold yourself up for a second and then release.

As you get accustomed to this exercise, you'll be able to feel your abdominals pull you up. **49**

Remember, the movement should be slow and controlled. Fast, jerky movements can lead to injury.

(Please note: My Ab-Isolator makes all abdominal exercises easier as it locks you onto target muscles.)

How NOT to do abdominal curls.

COMMON MISTAKES: I'll bet if I asked you to do this exercise without first explaining the proper technique, you would lie down, place your feet together, put your hands behind your head, and yank yourself up with your arms. You would be wrenching your neck and could end up injuring your neck or back. And you wouldn't be working your abdominals at all. Your effort would be a waste of time, a waste of energy, and would contribute nothing at all to the gorgeous body you want to shape.

PAUL AVALONE

Cleveland, Ohio

In 1989 Paul Avalone, a thirty-one-year-old police officer, was in terrible shape. He weighed 370 pounds and had chronic back pain as a result of arthritis in his spine. The pain was so bad that just getting in and out of his squad car was an ordeal. To make matters worse, after a bout of pneumonia he developed asthma. His doctor advised him to lose weight as a way of controlling the asthma and to ease constant back pain. All told, Paul was feeling pretty sorry for himself:

"I stayed up late the night the doctor told me how much weight I had to lose. Flipping through the TV channels, I came across Tony telling his life story and advertising one of his exercise videos. Tony looked great, and he came across as so positive that I called and ordered the tape. But when it came, I put it aside. A few weeks later, after eating enough lasagna for three or four people at my birthday dinner, I promised myself to start eating properly and exercising daily.

"I was so fat that I could hardly bend in the middle to do abdominal curls, but I pushed myself through at least the beginner's stage of each of the exercises. When I began, I was kind of doubtful that I would have the perseverance to meet my goals, but I kept hearing Tony say things like 'You can do it' and 'It's attitude, folks.' So I just did it. Now I weigh 185 pounds. I lost half my body weight in one year! My asthma is all but gone, and my back no longer hurts. I can do things now that I couldn't do when I was twenty."

WORKING WITH WEIGHT

When you can easily do two sets at the advanced level, you can add weight to your workout. You don't necessarily need to buy dumbbells. Use a heavy book (three to five pounds) or anything else you can hold easily while you exercise. When the exercise is easy with weight, add more in increments of three to five pounds. Don't sacrifice technique for added weight. No amount of weight will help if your technique isn't perfect.

Exercise #2

●

REVERSE TORSO CURLS

This exercise for your lower midriff tones and strengthens the frontal and lower abdominal muscles (the rectus abdominals and transverse abdominals). It's terrific for your whole abdominal area, but because most of the resistance comes from the lower body instead of the upper body, reverse torso curls help tighten your lower abdominals somewhat more than the upper abs. This exercise helps men and women in slightly different ways. Women carry most of their fat cells in their lower midsection, hips, buttocks, and thighs, while men carry their fat higher, in the upper and lateral part of the midsection. Either way, reverse torso curls are going to help transform your abdominal area. You will be firm, tight, and toned to the bone.

- Lie on the floor, arms at your sides and your palms flat on the floor for support.

- Dig your buttocks into the floor.

- Raise your legs as shown in picture A. Your knees should be slightly bent, your ankles crossed. *If you have a back problem, you'll probably be more comfortable if you bend your knees so that your lower legs are at a right angle to your thighs.* Be sure to keep your knees above (in alignment with) your hips.

- Squeeze your abdominal muscles to raise your legs as shown in picture B. This is a very small movement. You're just tilting up your pelvis. Never swing your legs back to get the lift, and don't raise your hips off the floor. *Think* about the movement and the muscles you're working. If you don't feel the effort in the right place, adjust your position so that you can feel it.

A

B

NEVER *do reverse torso curls this way!*

CARTER KIMBEL

Exeter, New Hampshire

Carter Kimbel is one cool dude, isn't he?

He made that change in himself by following my program and taking my advice about low-fat eating.

Carter, who is five feet six inches tall, weighed 190 pounds when he decided to get in shape. He dropped thirty pounds and got rid of his gut in six months.

"I haven't looked or felt this good since I came out of the service in 1968," he wrote me. "I no longer have to walk around holding my stomach in, which makes me feel super. I tried other systems before, but nothing beats your program for quick results. I noticed a difference in only a week or so. The stomach routine makes you feel strong all over."

WILFRED THIBODEAN

Jacksonville, Florida

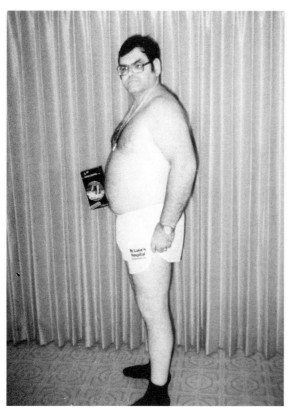 

Where did Wilfred's gut go?

He was in pretty sad shape when he began my program in March 1992: "I weighed 215 pounds and was always tired. My blood pressure and cholesterol levels were too high. I had tried many diets and exercise programs, but I always failed. I'd been overweight for twenty-nine years. And I didn't think I could lose weight because in my job I serve pastries and other fattening foods every day.

"After watching your tapes, I began to believe I could get in shape. I started with a forty-six-inch chest, forty-six-inch waist, and forty-four-inch hips. By June 1992 I'd lost forty-five pounds and twenty-four inches. My chest is now forty-one inches, my waist is thirty-five inches, and my hips are thirty-six inches. My blood pressure and cholesterol are now normal."

Wilfred says he wants to lose ten more pounds. Now that he knows how to get results, I'm betting that he'll succeed.

Exercise #3

●

OBLIQUE CURLS

This exercise looks harder than it is. In fact, if it feels as if you are doing no movement at all, you're probably doing oblique curls perfectly. You'll be working the internal and external oblique muscles, which wrap around your midsection like a corset and support you laterally. Men need this exercise to get rid of their "love handles" and strengthen their midsections. Women need it to define the waist.

- Lie down, knees bent, feet flat on the floor at shoulder width.

- Place your right hand on your head just above your ear, as the model is doing in picture A.

- Pull yourself up as you would for abdominal curls.
  Once you're up, turn slightly toward your raised knee and *squeeze*. Picture C shows the correct position. *Don't push your elbow or head forward as you turn.* If you lead with your right shoulder, you'll get the effort you need.

- After you've finished with the left side, *repeat* this exercise for the muscles on your right side.

SAFETY TIP: Never twist your head when doing this exercise. If you do, you can hurt your neck. Look toward the ceiling, and remember to keep your head in neutral position.

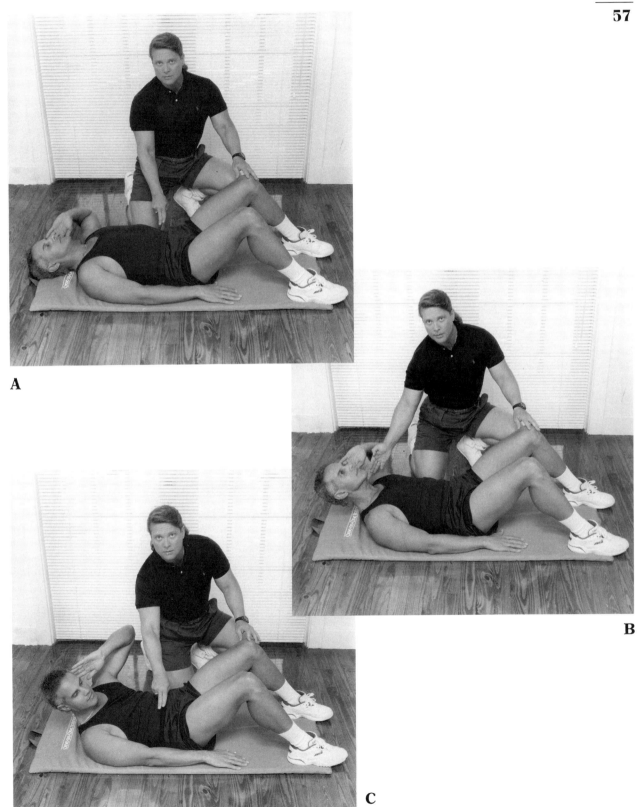

A

B

C

Exercise #4

●

BACK EXTENSIONS

This exercise for the erector spinae muscles in your lower back and the upper back will give you super muscles and make the whole area stronger. As a result, you'll have much better balance between your abdominal and back muscles. You also will have more upright posture and place much less strain on your back.

- Lie on your stomach, arms relaxed and at your sides.

- Your legs should be relaxed, too, with your knees slightly flexed.

- Relax your neck so that your head faces your exercise mat. Be sure not to pull your head back (hyperextend) during this exercise.

- Tense your buttocks and pull in your abdominal muscles. Picture **A** shows the correct starting position.

- Now, pull your chest off the floor by contracting the muscles in your lower back (see picture **B**). Don't worry about how high you raise yourself. All you need is a small movement and a big *squeeze*. Hold yourself up for a moment before releasing your muscles.

You can add weight only after you can easily do two sets at the advanced level. Hug the added weight to your chest while you do the movement. Be sure to keep your head in neutral position—don't hyperextend. Add three to five pounds at first, and then add more weight as the exercise becomes easier. *Never* try to do this exercise with more than fifteen pounds of added weight. You could hurt your back, and you would be very mad at me.

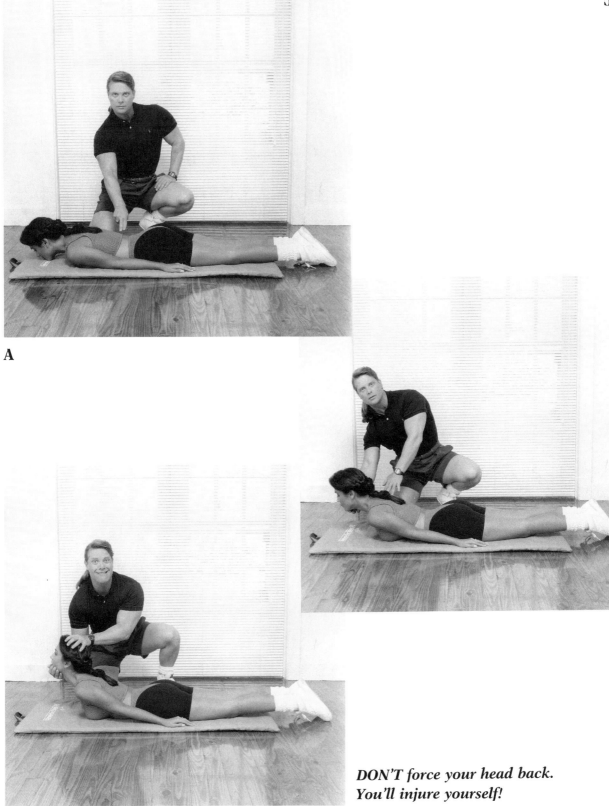

A

B

***DON'T force your head back.
You'll injure yourself!***

60   COOLDOWN

After you've finished your abdominal workout, cool down by repeating your favorite stretches from pages 41–45.

Great job. You're on your way to a perfect body and a positive attitude.

Use the chart below to keep track of your progress this week. Perfect your technique and you soon will see and feel an improvement.

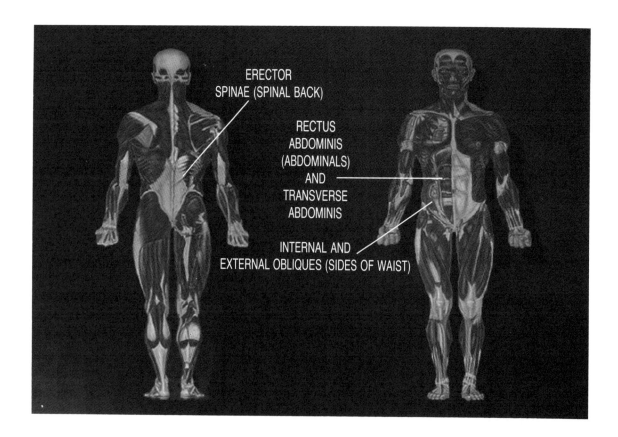

ERECTOR
SPINAE (SPINAL BACK)

RECTUS
ABDOMINIS
(ABDOMINALS)
AND
TRANSVERSE
ABDOMINIS

INTERNAL AND
EXTERNAL OBLIQUES (SIDES OF WAIST)

The abdominals and back are the muscles you're working on this week.

WEEK ONE:
ABDOMINAL REDUCTION, BACK AND ABDOMINAL STRENGTHENING WORKOUT

FIVE DAYS PER WEEK

NOTE: Don't forget your active warmup and static stretching before your workout.

Date: 4-3-95										
Abdominal Workout	Monday		Tuesday		Wednesday		Thursday		Friday	
	Reps	Sets	Reps	Sets	Reps	Sets	Reps	Sets	Reps	Sets
Exercise #1 Abdominal Curls	8	1								
Exercise #2 Reverse Torso Curls	8	1								
Exercise #3 Oblique Curls	8	1								
Exercise #4 Back Extensions	8	1								

Beginner 6–8 Repetitions (1 Set)	Intermediate 9–15 Repetitions (1 Set)	Advanced 16–25 Repetitions (1 Set)

Repetitions: The number of times you do a particular exercise before stopping.
Set: One round of repetitions per exercise.

Women who are generally looking for fat reduction and a shapely, well-toned body should use higher repetitions and low weight resistance.
Men who are generally looking for fat reduction and building a muscular, athletic-looking physique use lower repetitions and heavier weights.

Example:
Intermediate Female—9–15 reps × 1 set of a given exercise with 3–5-pound dumbbells.
Example:
Intermediate Male—9–15 reps × 1 set of a given exercise with 10–15-pound dumbbells or heavier, but never sacrificing *technique* for heavier weight.

Abdominal Exercise
1. Abdominal Curls
2. Reverse Torso Curls
3. Oblique Curls
Back Exercise
1. Back Extension

Don't forget to properly hydrate yourself (drink water) before and during exercise as you need it.

Always Concentrate on Technique! Technique Is the Key to
Safe and Effective Results.

4
Week Two:
LOWER BODY WORKOUT

This week you're going to begin to strengthen some of your body's biggest muscles. You'll also continue to do your abdominal and back workout Monday through Friday. But on Monday, Wednesday, and Friday you will add a new set of exercises for your legs, hips, and buttocks. Use the chart on pages 92–93 to record the number of repetitions you do each day for both sets of exercises.

Altogether you'll be working on six large muscles in your buttocks and hips, the fronts and backs of your upper legs, and the fronts and backs of your lower legs (the diagrams on page 93 give you a back and front view of the muscles). Regardless of whether your legs are skinny or fat, if they're weak, you never will have a strong, balanced foundation on which to build a strong, shapely body. Your legs are a visible indication of how fit you are. The lower body workout also counteracts the dreaded "droopy buttock syndrome" that afflicts couch potatoes of both sexes. Within two weeks you should begin to feel and see a difference in your body. I give you my word.

WHAT YOU NEED

You'll need some of the same equipment you used for your abdominal and back body exercises:

- The exercise mat or padding
- A chair for balance
- The workout gear and athletic shoes

You'll also need some weights: three- to five-pound dumbbells for women; ten to fifteen pounds for men.

64   WARMING UP

I can't overstress the importance of a five-minute active warm-up. It is essential to prevent injuries. Getting the blood flowing to the muscles you'll be using warms them up so that they're supple, flexible, and most efficient. So let's go put on some music and start to move and groove!

Warming up is crucial to a successful, injury-free workout.

TRAIN HARD! THINK COOL! LOOK HOT!

Remember: Don't exert yourself during the warm-up. Try to work up a light sweat by moving to the music.

- Shake your hips.
- March to the music.
- Dance around the room if you like.
- Swing your arms back and forth.
- Do a few easy squats—just bend your knees and pretend you're going to sit down. Have fun!

STRETCHING

This week you're going to add to the stretches you learned last week for your abdominal workout. Remember to *repeat* the stretches during your cooldown to help your muscles recover from the physical stress of the workout and help prevent cramping. All told, these should take from three to five minutes—time well spent.

Hold each stretch for ten counts.

1. *Low back and hamstring stretch* (for the erector spinae and hamstring muscles in your lower back and the backs of your legs): Slowly lower yourself to the floor. Lying on your back, bend your right leg, then raise it and pull it gently toward your chest, as shown in picture C. Slowly lower it and repeat with the left leg.

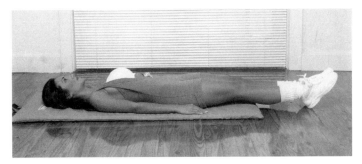

A

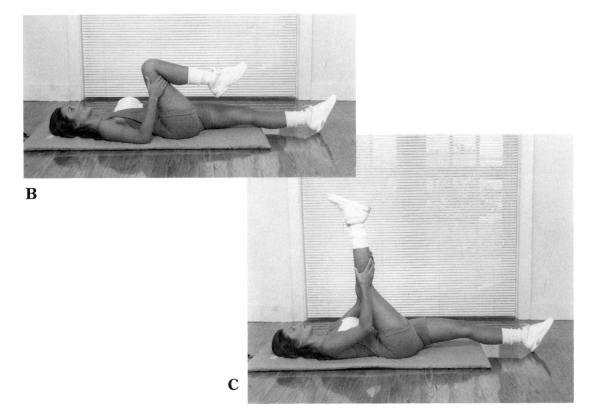

B

C

66   **2.** *Lateral low back and quadriceps stretch* (for your low back, abdominals, and shoulders, as well as for the quadriceps in the front of the upper leg): You first stretch back, abs, and shoulders, then quads. Lying on your right side, bend your left leg at the knee and stretch it toward the floor as shown in picture A. At the same time, stretch your left arm in the opposite direction as far as you can. Then slowly reach down and pull up your ankle to stretch the front of your thigh. As your flexibility increases, you'll be able to go farther. Repeat, lying on your left side.

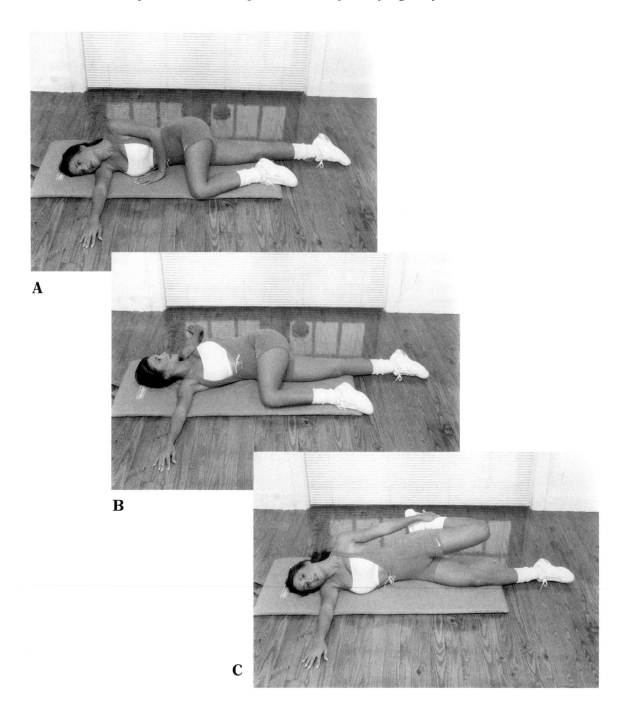

A

B

C

3. *Full back and hip stretch* (for your legs, back, hips, and buttocks): Sit back on or between your heels, then stretch your chest and arms out on the floor in front of you as shown in picture B. Stretch only as far as you can without discomfort.

A

B

A

B

4. *Lunge stretch* (for hips and the front and back of your upper legs): Place your left foot in front of you and lean into a kneeling position, though your knee shouldn't quite touch the floor (see picture B). You should feel the stretch in the front and back of your left thigh, the front of your right, and in your hips. Repeat the stretch for your right leg.

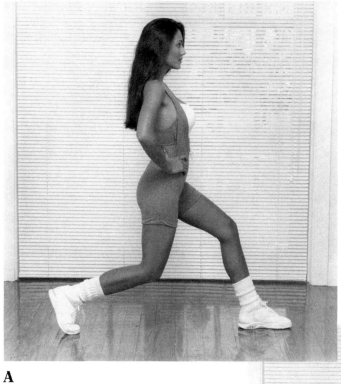

A

B

5. *Calf stretch* (for your lower legs): Standing up, place your left leg in front of your right. Rest your heel on the floor and raise your toes. Bend your right knee as shown in picture A. Then press your heel to the floor. You should feel the stretch in the back of your left thigh (the hamstring muscle) and calf. Repeat the stretch for your right leg.

70

6. *Lateral neck stretch* (for the muscles in the sides of your neck): While standing up, stretch your head to the right as if you were trying to touch your ear to your shoulder (see picture B). Do this stretch gently. Do not force your head down. Repeat for the left side.

A

B

C

7. *Frontal and posterior neck stretch* (for your neck and back): Stretch your neck by bending your head toward the floor. Then raise your chin until you feel the front of your neck stretching. Do this gently without forcing it.

Now that you've done your stretching you may begin your workout with confidence. You'll get a more productive workout without injury.

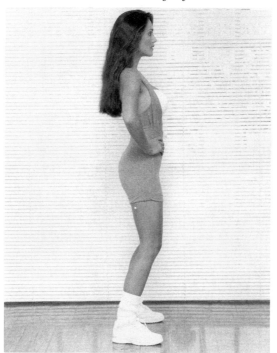

A

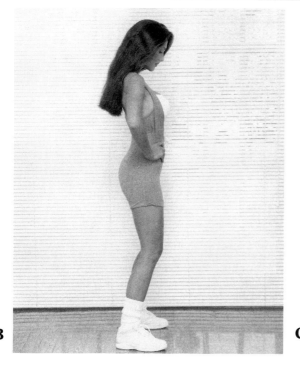

B

C

72 PACING YOURSELF

> **REMINDER:** Regardless of your exercise history, begin at the beginner's level and do not advance until you have mastered exercise technique.

- *Beginners:* six to eight reps (one set)
- *Intermediate:* nine to fifteen reps (one set)
- *Advanced:* sixteen to twenty-five reps (one set)
  (Do two sets if not challenged.)

Remember, advance from the beginner's level when you can easily do all the repetitions in one set, your technique is perfect, and your workout is no longer challenging. At the advanced level you'll begin adding weight after you can complete two sets and two consecutive workouts have been easy.

When you start to use weight, go back to the intermediate level. Work your way back up to two sets at the advanced level. When your workout becomes easy you can increase the amount of weight you use. But go back to the intermediate level again. You don't need to buy dumbbells at first. You can use a heavy book or any other household object weighing five pounds or less (weigh the book or whatever you decide to use on the bathroom scale). Never add more than five pounds at a time. At first, an extra two or three pounds will make a big difference, so don't be in a hurry to add a lot of weight.

Don't rush through your exercises. Quality (doing them correctly) is more important than quantity. Concentrate on technique. Once you're in the habit of doing the exercises properly, you'll find you can easily do more repetitions and advance from one level to another.

TECHNIQUE, TECHNIQUE, TECHNIQUE

You'll be doing some of the lower body exercises while standing and some on the floor. Before you begin, make sure your form is correct and your back is protected. If you have back problems or weakness, use a weight belt to insure proper form (see photo on the next page).

- Place your feet slightly wider than your shoulders.
- Flex your knees.
- Tighten your thigh muscles.
- Pull in your abdominal muscles and keep them tight throughout your workout.
- Hold your chest up.
- Hold your back straight with your shoulders pulled back slightly.
- Hold your head in neutral position. Make sure there's no tension in your neck.

THE WORKOUT

All of the exercises that follow as well as those in chapters 3 and 5 are numbered in sequence. Chapter 3 contained exercises #1 through #4. This chapter contains exercises #5 through #11.

Exercise #5

●

MODIFIED SQUATS

This exercise works three different sets of muscles: the quadriceps in the front of the thigh, the gluteals (the muscles in your buttocks), and the biceps femoris, or "hamstrings," in back of your upper legs. You will get great leg development out of this movement if you do it correctly.

- Check for proper body alignment: feet shoulder width apart or wider in the beginning if it's not comfortable or if your legs are long, abdominals pulled in, chest up, shoulders retracted, head in neutral position.

- Place your hands on your hips if you're not working with weights. If you're working with weights, hold them at shoulder level. Pictures A and B show the proper starting position with and without weights.

- Bend your knees and squat as shown in pictures C and D. As you squat, take your hands off your hips and raise them in front of you. This will give you better balance as you go down. You don't have to squat as low as the model in the picture. Go as low as you comfortably can. Make sure your knees are lined up with your big and second toes. You'll get the movement right if you pretend you're about to sit down: stick out your buttocks as if there were a chair behind you. You may feel silly but the results are best this way.

- Keep your abdominals tight, and *squeeze* your buttocks and thighs as you come back to the starting position. Be sure that you don't lock your knees when you straighten up.

- Repeat until you've completed your set(s).

Squeeze . . . squeeze . . . squeeze! So you can tease . . . tease . . . tease!

TIP #1: If you wobble or feel unstable as you begin to squat, take a wider stance and place a rolled towel or your folded mat under your heels. It will help stabilize you, give you better balance and support, and allow for better range of motion.

A

B

C

D

TIP #2: Don't look straight up as you squat. You could hyperextend your neck and injure yourself. Keep your head in the neutral position with slight eye elevation.

Exercise #6

●

WIDE STANCE SQUATS

Wide stance squats shape, tone, and strengthen the fronts and backs of the thighs (the quadriceps femoris and bicep femoris, or hamstrings), as well as your buttock muscles (gluteal muscles).

For wide stance squats, stand with your feet farther apart than they were during modified squats. You won't need a towel or mat to prevent wobbling because your stance is wider and you'll be more stable.

- Stand with your hands on your hips and your feet wider than your shoulders. Make sure your knees are slightly flexed, your abdominals are pulled in tight, your chest is pulled up, shoulders back and your head is in neutral position, as shown in picture A.

- Place your hands on your hips and squat slowly, squeezing your buttocks and thigh muscles as you come back up. Think about it. Don't just go through the motions. You don't have to squat as low as the model in picture B.

  Never drop below knee level as the model is doing in picture C, or you'll paint the wall with your kneecaps.

- Come back to the starting position. As you come up, *squeeze* the muscles in your thighs. Concentrate on your movement. Keep your mind on your thighs if you want results.

- Repeat until you have completed your set(s).

A

B

C

DON'T drop below knee level!

EILEEN GILLARD

Marquette, Missouri

Eileen Gillard first wrote me in August of 1992. You can see the incredible change in her body. How did she do it? I'm going to let her speak for herself.

"After getting married and having three children, I became a couch potato. I kept putting on weight and gave up all forms of exercise, even dancing. I was fat and lazy and so embarrassed by my appearance that I never wanted to see friends and family. My "before" photo is the only one I have of the way I looked then, because when you get as big as I was, you try to stay away from cameras.

"November 1, 1991, was the worst day of my life. My husband told me I was fat, ugly, and repulsive to him, and then he walked out on me.

"That same day I found Tony Little, the best thing that ever happened to me. Tony gave me back my figure, but more than that, he helped me build my self-esteem and made me laugh when my life was otherwise falling apart.

"Since I've been following Tony's exercise programs, I've never been tired, and I've never been more energetic. I haven't been dieting, but I do try to choose the right foods and cut down on fats. I've lost fifty-five pounds and plan to lose fifteen more. My children, Jeremy, Amanda, and Lisa, are so proud of me, and it makes me feel good to be setting a healthy example for them."

MICHAEL A. LEVY

Cooper City, Florida

What a transformation in Mike Levy!

Because Mike considers himself a klutz, he never exercised. He was more than fifty pounds overweight and very self-conscious about his body. When he first started using one of my workout tapes, his waist measured thirty-eight inches and his chest forty-four inches. Since then he has lost nine inches from his waist and six from his chest.

Not only does Mike look different, he *feels* different: "When I was in my thirties I felt as though I were fifty-something. Today, at fifty-one, I feel like a thirty-year-old. I've lost weight, toned up, and have infinitely more energy than ever before in my life."

Here's more from Mike's letters:

"By nature, I'm a very skeptical person who believes that few products fully live up to the claims and promises that come with them. I suspected that this workout program probably would be one more disappointment. I couldn't have been more wrong. It has helped me achieve goals I've dreamed about all my life.

"I never would have believed what this program could do for me if I hadn't seen it for myself."

Exercise #7
●
LUNGES

Lunges strengthen and tone the muscles in the fronts of your thighs (the quadriceps femoris), hip flexors, the sides of your hips, the muscles in the backs of your thighs (the biceps femoris, or hamstrings), and your buttocks (gluteal muscles). Eventually you'll be doing this exercise with weights, but not until you are confident of your technique and balance. Once the advanced level becomes easy, men can add ten to fifteen pounds, women three to five pounds.

Your stance for this exercise is a modification of proper body alignment: tight abs, chest out, shoulders back.

- Stand with your right leg in front of your left. Your legs should be wide apart but not so wide that your left foot isn't planted firmly on the floor. Check pictures A and B for the correct starting stance. Your most important consideration is to have a strong, confident back first. Despite the placement of your legs, the other elements of proper body alignment are the same.

- Your knees are slightly flexed.

- Your thigh and buttocks muscles are tight.

- Your abdominals are pulled tight.

- Your chest is high, your shoulder blades retracted, and your head is in neutral position with no tension in your neck.

- If you're using weights, hold them at your side as shown.

- Keeping all your muscles tight, slowly lower your left knee toward the floor, as shown in pictures C and D. You don't have to go down as far as the model. Lower your knee only as far as you can without losing your balance or sacrificing technique.

- As you bend your left leg, glance down to make sure that your right knee does not extend beyond the end of your right foot.

- *Squeeze* your buttocks and legs as you come back to the starting position. The lunge should be a slow, controlled movement, keeping all your muscles tight. You should feel the effort in the upper thigh.

Repeat the sequence with your left leg in front.

A

B

C

D

Exercise #8

●

HIP ABDUCTION (ALTERNATE LEG RAISES)

You do this exercise lying on your floor mat. You'll be toning and strengthening the abductor muscles on the outside of your upper legs. In combination with aerobic activity, this great shaping exercise can help women get rid of the "saddlebags" on their upper thighs. But doing it correctly is a lot harder than it looks. A common mistake, particularly among women, is to raise the working leg too high as the model is demonstrating in the picture. You can't lift your leg that high without rolling back on your hips. The result is that you aren't working your muscles, you're just showing off how flexible you are. Women are a lot more flexible than men in the hip area. They have to be for childbearing. This exercise requires a lot of concentration, so study the pictures on page 83 carefully and make sure you follow instructions to the letter.

- Lie down on your right side. Extend your right arm out on the floor and rest your head on your arm as shown in picture A.

- Place your legs at a 90-degree angle to your trunk as if you were sitting on a chair.

- Now, slowly slide your legs out to a 45-degree angle to your body. Keep your knees together, your hips stable and still. Don't let yourself roll back or forward. Keeping your abdominal muscles tight will prevent any movement.

- Keeping your knees together, extend your top leg out in front of you.

- Your right foot should be flexed and facing front.

- Now, slowly raise and lower your top leg as shown in picture B. The effort should come from the muscles in your outer thigh, and the movement itself should be very short. Don't swing your leg up and down. Lift and lower using the abductor muscles.

Once the advanced level becomes easy, you can add weight. Hold a dumbbell in the middle of your thigh as shown in the picture. For more resistance, move the weight closer to your knee. Women can add three to five pounds. Since men find this exercise harder than women, I suggest using the same amount of weight (three to five pounds).

- Repeat the exercise until you've completed your set(s). Then repeat for the left leg.

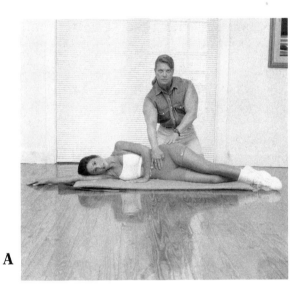

A

B

C

How you SHOULDN'T do a leg raise!

Exercise #9

●

HIP ADDUCTION (INNER THIGH)

Now you're going to work on the muscles of your inner thigh (the adductors). You'll be toning, strengthening, and eliminating the jiggly flesh that is a problem for many women. Since men tend to have firmer inner thighs than women, you would think that this exercise would be easier for men than women. But it isn't. At least, it's a tough one for me.

You're still on the floor for this exercise.

- Lie on your left side with your left arm extended and your head resting on your arm.

- Bend your right (top) leg and rest it on the floor in front of you as shown in picture A. This reduces some of the tightness in the lower back and hips as you perform the exercise. If you're not comfortable in the position, place a folded towel under your knee as the model is doing in the picture.

- Check to make sure that your bent knee is aligned with your right hip and that your hips are aligned with your shoulders as they would be if you were standing up with proper body alignment. Be sure your abdominals are pulled in tight.

- *Squeezing* your inner thigh muscles, raise your lower leg and then lower it as shown in picture B. This is a short movement. Go only as high as you can without moving your hips. Your foot should be level. Don't let it rotate so that your toes point to the floor or ceiling.

- You can add weight after your workout becomes easy. Rest a dumbbell in the middle of your working thigh. But remember, never sacrifice exercise technique for weight.

- Repeat until you have completed your set(s). Then repeat for your other leg.

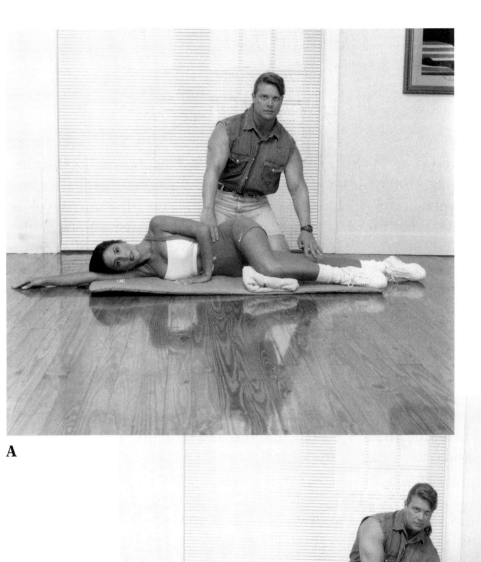

A

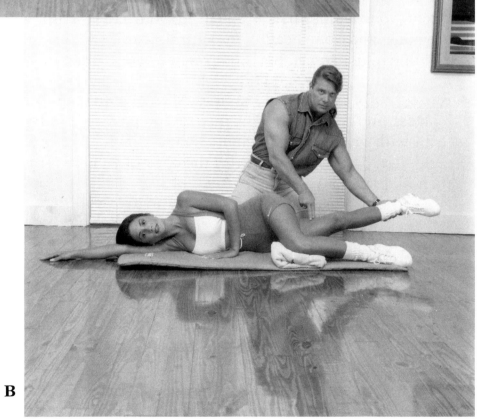

B

Exercise #10

●

HEEL RAISES

You have to stand up to do this exercise for your calves. If you do it right, you'll feel it the first time you try it, but in time it will tone the gastrocnemius and soleus muscles in the backs of your lower legs so that you develop a nice heart shape, which is so sexy when women are wearing high heels. If you glance down at your calves as you do this exercise, you'll be able to see the muscles in action and get a preview of how your legs are going to look.

For balance, you can hold on to the back of a stable chair or another piece of furniture as you do this exercise. Eventually you'll be holding dumbbells, but since proper technique is as important here as it is for any of the other exercises, learn to do it right before adding weight.

- Check yourself for proper body alignment. Make sure your knees are flexed, your abdominals are held in, your chest is up, your shoulders are back, and your head is in neutral position.

  If you're using weights, hold them at your sides as shown.

- Raise your heels off the floor, hold, *squeeze* with your lower leg muscles (calves), and then lower. The pictures on pages 87 and 88 show proper form with and without weight. Lower slowly. If you want more of a challenge, do this exercise with the back of your foot resting on a two-inch high towel or board.

You probably will feel your calf muscles start to burn as you do this. You may have to stop and start again.

TIP: If you're holding on to a chair while doing heel raises, you can put a two-by-four under the ball of your feet so your heels can get more range of motion. This will help build your calves more quickly by stretching your calves out during each repetition.

PATTI

For professional reasons, Patti asked me not to use her last name or tell you where she lives, but she did give me permission to use her pictures and tell you her remarkable story.

Her "before" photo was taken at a barbecue in February 1993. Patti, who is five feet three inches, weighed 220 pounds. Here is what she wrote: "Needless to say, I wasn't real happy about my size, but after being on many diets over the years and after regaining what I had lost more times than I remember, I was at the point where it was impossible to lose weight, regardless of how little I ate. I'd given up trying to change the way I looked and had taken up dressing to blend in with the walls." Then she saw me on television and decided to order one of my tapes, figuring that she would return it for her money back when it didn't work.

Because of an injury, she wasn't able to begin working out until February 1993. Over the next seven months Patti lost ninety pounds. Her measurements went from 48-42-50 to 37-27-37. She also lost six inches from each thigh and five inches around each calf.

"I can't tell you how much my attitude and life have changed," Patti says. She even suggested that I warn people that "if you use this method, your clothes will never fit properly again . . . they'll be *too big*."

Exercise #11

●

ALTERNATE TOE RAISES

Very few exercise programs pay attention to the muscles in the front of the lower leg (the tibialis anterior). But if you have any ankle problems, you'll find that strengthening this muscle will make a big difference. And it will add a really pretty shape to the lower legs.

Like the heel raises, this exercise looks a lot easier than it is. It also brings on that nasty burn.

- Stand with your right leg in front of your left, resting your hands on your right thigh as the model is doing in picture A. Both of your knees should be flexed.

- Check for proper body alignment: abdominals tight, chest up, head in neutral position.

- Raise and lower the toes of your right foot as shown in picture B. The object is to *squeeze* as your toes come up as high as possible without losing your balance. Concentrate on *technique*.

- Repeat the exercise using your left foot.

You're going to feel this exercise in the top and front of your lower leg. You may have to stop and start again to complete all your repetitions.

That's it for your lower body resistance exercise program.

A

B

92   COOLDOWN

Begin your cooldown just by walking around for two to three minutes. Swing your arms. Don't exert any effort. Your movements should be loose and easy.

Turn back to pages 65–71 and repeat a few of the stretches. Choose your favorites. You'll be sorry if you skip this part of your workout. Stretching helps your muscles recover and prevents soreness.

Tomorrow you'll do your abdominal and back exercises. You'll repeat your lower body workout on alternate days for the rest of the week. Do the workout three times.

That's the end of your lower body exercises for today. You conceived of a great body. You now believe you can do it. And you will.

Next week you will begin to work your upper body. The other half.

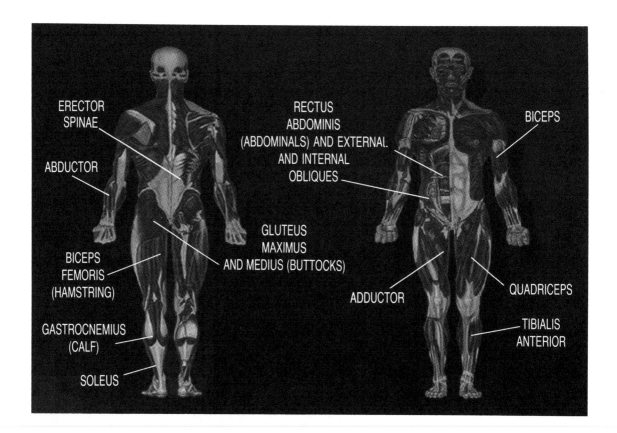

The muscles you're exercising this week.

WEEK TWO:
ABDOMINAL, BACK, AND
LOWER BODY WORKOUT

NOTE: Don't forget your active warmup and static stretching before your workout.

DATE:				DATE:				DATE:			
MONDAY Abdominal, Back, Lower Body Workout				**TUESDAY** Abdominal, Back, Lower Body Workout				**WEDNESDAY** Abdominal, Back, Lower Body Workout			
	WEIGHT	REPS	SET(S)		WEIGHT	REPS	SET(S)		WEIGHT	REPS	SET(S)
Exercise #1 Abdominal Curls				Exercise #1 Abdominal Curls				Exercise #1 Abdominal Curls			
Exercise #2 Reverse Torso Curls				Exercise #2 Reverse Torso Curls				Exercise #2 Reverse Torso Curls			
Exercise #3 Oblique Curls				Exercise #3 Oblique Curls				Exercise #3 Oblique Curls			
Exercise #4 Back Extensions				Exercise #4 Back Extensions				Exercise #4 Back Extensions			
Exercise #5 Modified Squats				Exercise #5 Modified Squats				Exercise #5 Modified Squats			
Exercise #6 Wide Stance Squats				Exercise #6 Wide Stance Squats				Exercise #6 Wide Stance Squats			
Exercise #7 Lunges (RT & LT)				Exercise #7 Lunges (RT & LT)				Exercise #7 Lunges (RT & LT)			
Exercise #8 Hip Abduction				Exercise #8 Hip Abduction				Exercise #8 Hip Abduction			
Exercise #9 Hip Adduction				Exercise #9 Hip Adduction				Exercise #9 Hip Adduction			
Exercise #10 Heel Raises				Exercise #10 Heel Raises				Exercise #10 Heel Raises			
Exercise #11 Alternate Toe Raises				Exercise #11 Alternate Toe Raises				Exercise #11 Alternate Toe Raises			

DATE:				DATE:			
THURSDAY Abdominal, Back, Lower Body Workout				**FRIDAY** Abdominal, Back, Lower Body Workout			
	WEIGHT	REPS	SET(S)		WEIGHT	REPS	SET(S)
Exercise #1 Abdominal Curls				Exercise #1 Abdominal Curls			
Exercise #2 Reverse Torso Curls				Exercise #1 Reverse Torso Curls			
Exercise #3 Oblique Curls				Exercise #3 Oblique Curls			
Exercise #4 Back Extensions				Exercise #4 Back Extensions			
Exercise #5 Modified Squats				Exercise #5 Modified Squats			
Exercise #6 Wide Stance Squats				Exercise #6 Wide Stance Squats			
Exercise #7 Lunges (RT & LT)				Exercise #7 Lunges (RT & LT)			
Exercise #8 Hip Abduction				Exercise #8 Hip Abduction			
Exercise #9 Hip Adduction				Exercise #9 Hip Adduction			
Exercise #10 Heel Raises				Exercise #10 Heel Raises			
Exercise #11 Alternate Toe Raises				Exercise #11 Alternate Toe Raises			

Beginner 6–8 Repetitions (1 Set)	Intermediate 9–15 Repetitions (1 Set)	Advanced 16–25 Repetitions (1 Set)

Option: Add another set if one is not challenging enough.

When technique is not perfect discontinue the exercise.
Do not go for more reps!
Remember, technique is the key to safe and effective results.

ABDOMINAL EXERCISES:
  1. Abdominal Curls
  2. Reverse Torso Curls
  3. Oblique Curls

BACK EXERCISE:
  4. Back Extensions

LOWER BODY EXERCISES:
  5. Modified Squats
  6. Wide Stance Squats
  7. Lunges (right and left)
  8. Hip Abduction
  9. Hip Adduction
  10. Heel Raises
  11. Alternate Toe Raises

Hip Adduction   Hip Abduction

5
Week Three:
UPPER BODY WORKOUT

This week you'll begin to work on your upper body—your back, chest, shoulders, and arms. You'll add the upper body exercises to your abdominal and lower body exercises for your first total body workout.

The upper body workout rounds off your basic resistance training program. Men can relate easily to the need for building up the arms, shoulders, and chest—after all, the upper body is where most of male strength resides. Women tend to focus on their hips, buttocks, and thighs and don't fully appreciate the need for upper body strengthening.

Ladies, take a look in the mirror. Are your upper arms firm or flabby? Upper arms usually are nice and firm until you reach your thirties. Then, watch out! Since we don't use the triceps muscles in the back of the arm very often in routine activities, they're among the first to sag. And it isn't a pretty picture. Eventually the flesh just dangles down from the bone. These "granny arms" are a big problem for women as they get older. But not for you. By working your triceps muscles, you're going to replace the flab with a nice, firm, youthful shape.

Bra bulge is another upper body problem for women. The loose flesh under the bra line is similar to the "love handles" men get at the waist.

Whether you're a man or a woman, you should see a V taper in the back and muscle definition in your arms. I'm not suggesting that your goal should be the well-developed bulging muscles bodybuilders have. I'm talking about shape, contour, and the visual beauty of your body. That comes when you burn fat away, reverse the ratio of muscle to fat in your favor, and replace granny arms with nicely toned muscles.

Beginning this week, you're also going to give your upper body a dynamic new look by strengthening and shaping your shoulder and chest muscles. I'm sure men have been looking forward to this part. I love having a dynamic body that looks and feels masculine. It gives me confidence that I can protect my family and myself in today's dangerous world.

Women may be doubtful that they need to work on the upper body. I hate to tell you, ladies, but if your shoulder and chest muscles aren't in shape, your breasts will start to, er, sag prematurely. But you can prevent that—with these exercises you can even reverse that! Here's another news flash for women: Once you build up and shape your shoulders, you can toss away your shoulder pads. Believe me, you won't need help to look great in (and out) of your clothes.

Within a few weeks of beginning to work these muscles, your body will start to change. When your muscles feel firmer and your clothes fit slightly different, you'll be witnessing the first sign of the beautiful new body that will soon emerge. And here's a bonus: Your everyday tasks will be easier because you'll be stronger and more flexible. Your metabolism will speed up as you replace flab with muscle, and you'll feel an incredible increase in your energy and more confidence. That is a physiological fact you can count on.

YOUR WORKOUT SCHEDULE

With the addition of upper body exercises to your program, you will be working out six days a week. At first you'll probably be able to do the entire workout within a half hour. Later, as you reach the advanced level and add weight to your workout, you'll be doing higher repetitions and more sets. As a result you probably will be spending more time exercising, but even an advanced workout shouldn't take an hour. That's how long my workout is. Doing the most amount of work in the shortest amount of time with the best technique gives you the greatest body. Look at me!

IMPORTANT: Never chat while you're working out. If you do, you'll lose your concentration. You'll sacrifice the benefits.

Here's your workout schedule for this week:
Monday-Wednesday-Friday: Lower body and upper body workout.
Tuesday-Thursday-Saturday: Abdominal and back exercises.
Use the chart on pages 140–141 to record your progress.

THE TOTAL RESISTANCE TRAINING PROGRAM

1. Abdominal curls
2. Reverse torso curls
3. Oblique curls
4. Back extensions

5. Modified squats
6. Wide stance squats
7. Lunges (right and left legs)
8. Hip abduction (alternate leg raises)
9. Hip adduction (inner thigh)
10. Heel raises
11. Alternate toe raises

12. Back rows
13. Chest presses
14. Chest flyes
15. Shoulder presses
16. Shoulder side raises
17. Shoulder frontal raises
18. Triceps extensions (or triceps kickback as substitute)
19. Alternate biceps curls (or concentration curl as substitute)
20. Zottman curls

FINDING YOUR LEVEL

As usual, I want you to begin at the beginner's level and advance only after you are sure your technique is perfect and you feel comfortable doing the exercises. After that, challenge yourself for a great body by moving from intermediate to advanced as soon as your workout is too easy for you. The same rule applies to working with weights: increase the amount whenever you can complete two sets at the advanced level *with perfect technique.* At that point go back to the intermediate level and add weight and work your way up to advanced.

Be sure to challenge yourself with every workout. When an exercise is easy to do, it isn't helping you.

- *Beginner:* six to eight reps (one set)
- *Intermediate:* ten to fifteen reps (one set)
- *Advanced:* sixteen to twenty-five reps (one set)
  (Do two sets at the advanced level if one set is too easy.)

GETTING READY

In addition to your workout gear, cross-training shoes, and the mat you've been using for your abdominal and lower body exercises, you'll need a set of hand weights (dumbbells) ranging in weight from three to five pounds for women and ten to fifteen pounds for men. You can get them in most sporting goods stores or order them from me. (See appendix 3 for ordering information.) When buying weights for home use, look for solid chrome or vinyl-coated iron dumbbells. Don't use big plastic disks—they're too clumsy. (The photos below show the right and wrong kinds of weight for home use.)

For one of your upper body workouts you'll also need a chair stable enough to support some of your weight.

These easy-to-handle, sleek weights are perfect for a great workout!

Clumsy, awkward and ugly plastic weights can hurt you!

WARMING UP

Since you'll be working your arms, chest, shoulders, and back, make sure to add the following movements to your active warm-up:

- Swing your arms back and forth.
- Bend your elbows and touch your fingers to your shoulders. These should be easy movements. You're just loosening up and warming these muscles—don't tense them.
- Shrug your shoulders.
- Roll your shoulders back three times.
- Roll your shoulders forward three times.

100   STRETCHING

This week you're going to add four new upper body stretches to ones you learned last week. I've marked the new ones with an asterisk (*).

Hold each stretch for *ten* slow counts.

1. *Low back and hamstring stretch:* Slowly lower yourself to the floor. Lying on your back, bend your right leg, then raise it. Pull it gently into your chest as shown in picture C. Make sure your hands are below, not above your knees.

A

B

C

A

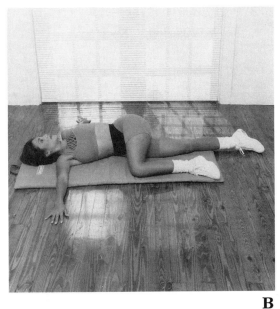

B

C

2. *Lateral low back and quadriceps stretch:* Lying on your right side, bend your left leg at the knee and stretch it toward the floor as shown in picture A. At the same time, stretch your left arm in the opposite direction as far as you comfortably can. Then slowly reach down and pull up your ankle to stretch the front of your thigh. Repeat lying on your left side.

102   **3.** *Full back and hip stretch:* Sit back on or between your heels, then stretch your chest and arms out on the floor in front of you as shown in picture B.

A

B

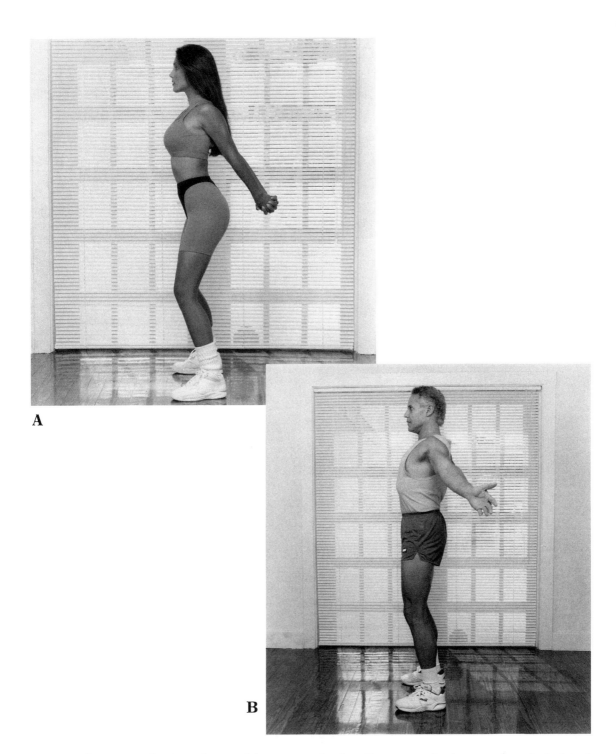

A

B

4. *Chest stretch:* Standing with proper body alignment, lock your hands behind your back and push your arms up as the model is doing in picture A. This is easier for women than men. If you can't lock your hands, just stretch your arms back with your palms facing front and push your arms back as the model is doing in picture B.

A

B

5. *Shoulder stretch:* Pull one arm across your chest and exert gentle pressure with the other arm as shown in picture A. Repeat for the other arm.

6. *Triceps stretch:* Reach your right arm up over your head. Grasp your right hand with your left and pull your arm toward the left shoulder as shown in picture A.

A

B

TECHNIQUE!

106   **7.** *Biceps stretch:* Reach your left hand behind your right elbow. Holding your right arm straight, stretch it back as the model is doing in picture A.

A

B

8. *Shrugs:* Standing with proper body alignment, hands on your hips, shrug your shoulders as the model is demonstrating in pictures A and B.

A

B

A

B

C

9. *Lateral neck stretch:* While standing up, stretch your head to the right as if you were trying to touch your ear to your shoulder. Do not force your head down. (See picture B.) Repeat for the left side.

10. *Frontal and posterior neck stretch:* Stretch your neck by bending your head toward the floor. Then raise your chin so that you feel the front of your neck stretching. This is a light stretch. Don't force your head down. (See pictures below.)

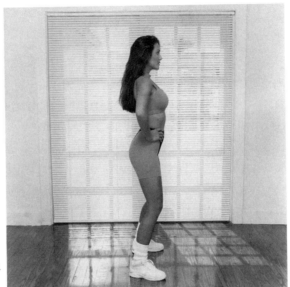

A

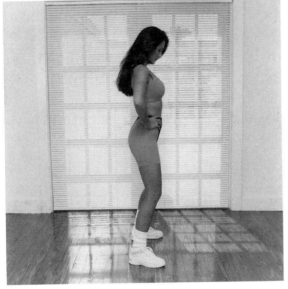

B

C

That's it for stretching. Now let's begin your workout.

THE WORKOUT

Remember the numbering system. Chapter 3 contained exercises #1 through #4. Chapter 4 contained exercises #5 through #11. This chapter contains exercises #12 through #20.

Exercise #12
●
BACK ROWS

This exercise works the large muscles of your back, the latissimus dorsi ("lats" for short), and some smaller, assisting back muscles. You'll be working with weight during this exercise as soon as you've mastered technique. Men can start with a ten- to fifteen-pound dumbbell; women can use three to five pounds. By working up to heavy weight (eight to ten reps), men can build a strong muscular back doing back rows. Women will do longer sets (fifteen or more reps) with lighter weights and achieve a beautiful V-shape taper that will make the waist look small and the chest perkier.

You can do this freestanding, using your leg for support as the model is doing in picture A. As you add weight, you'll need more support, so use a chair or bench as shown in picture C on page 113. If you have back problems, always use a chair or bench for support while doing this exercise.

- Rest the palm of your left hand on the seat of the chair as shown on page 113.

- Your knees should be slightly flexed, your abdominals pulled in tight, your buttocks contracted.

A

B

C

112

- Holding the weight in your right hand, pull up and back at a slight left angle. Your arm should be rounded as shown in picture D and your lats and chest perfectly balanced and parallel to the floor.

- *Squeeze* the weight up with your back muscles. If you're doing the movement properly, you'll feel the work in your shoulder blade and back. Isolate the back muscles to do the movement. Your arm and hand stay in the same position. Their only function is to hold the weight and create resistance. Try not to work with your arm.

- After each pull let your arm come all the way down so that you feel a slight stretch in the muscle you used. The stretch is as important as the pull. It adds length to the muscle to give it a better shape.

- Repeat the exercise for your left arm.

A

B

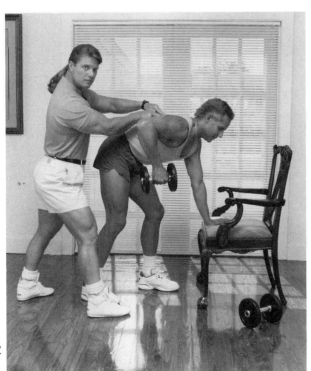

C

Exercise #13

●

CHEST PRESSES

This one is for your chest muscles (pectorals, or "pecs"), your shoulders (deltoids), and the triceps muscles in the back of your upper arm. Think about isolating your chest and shoulders. You can do this exercise lying on the floor or an exercise bench, if you have one.

Do this exercise without weights until you're sure you have the technique down pat. Then men can use ten- to fifteen-pound and women three- to five-pound dumbbells.

- I recommend an exercise bench for this, but it can be done on the floor. Be sure to place a rolled-up towel between your shoulder blades at the base of your neck. This will give you more range of motion as you move and will work the muscles more effectively.

116

- Lie on your back with your knees bent and feet flat on the floor.

- Bend your arms so that your elbows are parallel to your shoulders and your forearms are at right angles to your upper arms as shown in picture A.

- Check yourself for proper body alignment. Your lower back should be flush to the floor. Your abs should be tight, your legs braced, your chest up, and your shoulders back.

- Push the weights straight up so that your arms are extended directly over your shoulders as shown in picture B. Your movement should be slow and controlled. You should feel the effort in your chest, so make sure to squeeze at the top of the movement. Be careful not to lock your elbows. *The effort should come from your chest, not your arms.* Again, think about the muscles you're working. If you're not feeling it in your chest muscles you're doing something wrong.

- Lower your arms to the starting position.

SAFETY TIP: If you're lying on a bench, don't let your upper arms drop below shoulder level. If you do, you could injure your deltoids.

A

B

Exercise #14
●
CHEST FLYES

Here's another great exercise for your chest, shoulders, and triceps. Again, you'll be lying on your back on a bench or on the floor with a rolled-up towel between your shoulder blades (see picture A).

- Lie down with your knees bent, your feet flat on the floor.

- Make sure your legs are braced properly, your abs tight, and your lower back flush to the floor or bench.

- Hold your arms out above your chest at shoulder level as shown picture B. Your elbows should be slightly flexed.

- Pull your arms down as shown in picture C. This is your starting position. Make sure your movement is slow and controlled. You should feel the stretch in your chest. Slowly raise your arms back to the starting position by squeezing your chest muscles. You will feel this in all the right places if you pretend you're hugging an oak tree (or a very large person) as you raise your arms.

- If you're using a bench, be careful not to let your arms drop below shoulder level. You could injure your neck or shoulders if you do.

A

B

C

D

CAROLYN TOVAR

Valrico, Florida

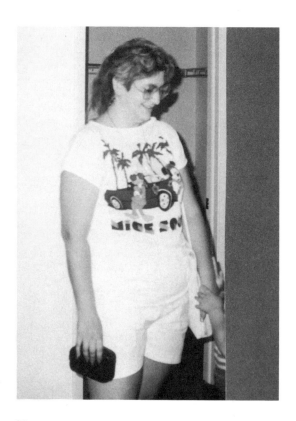

In January 1992 Carolyn Tovar burst out of a pair of size 16 jeans. At five feet five inches she weighed 195. "I was so disgusted with myself," she wrote. "I weighed a great big 195 pounds, major fat for someone my height."

Carolyn knew she had to lose weight, but since she'd been heavy all her life, she worried that her legs and butt would become flabby. Her mother sent for one of my workout tapes, and Carolyn went out and bought some books on low-fat eating. Here are some excerpts of her letter to me:

"I changed my eating habits and drank eight to ten glasses of water a day. When I received the tape, I started the exercise program. I've never been a workout-type person, but I really enjoyed the exercises. As the weeks went by, I went from size 16 jeans to 14, to 11–12 to 9–10, and by the end of April I was a size 5–6.

"I'm a new person. People I haven't seen since before I began to lose weight don't believe it when they see me. And they always comment on how tight my legs and butt are. They just can't believe that I'm not all flabby."

When Carolyn wrote to me in July of 1992 she weighed 130—an incredible sixty-five-pound loss from her starting weight of 195 in January 1992! And she asked about an upper body workout for her arms, "the only place that I have flab, and I don't like it."

Exercise #15

●

SHOULDER PRESSES

This exercise works your shoulder muscles (deltoids). Eventually you're going to use weight.

WARNING: Do *not* use weight if you have high blood pressure unless you have your doctor's approval. Squeezing weights can adversely affect your pressure. Even with a doctor's approval, use weights only if you are able to maintain a light grip. Or simply use no weight at all and work out with open hands.

Women should start with three- to five-pound dumbbells; men can use ten to fifteen pounds. If the exercise is too difficult or tiring with the weights, do it without them until you build up some strength. But do a few repetitions with weights before putting them down, and try to increase the number of reps with weights each time you exercise. You'll be surprised at how quickly you gain strength and feel your body firming up. In time you'll find that you can do more and more repetitions with weights. Remember the rule about advancing from one level to another: Don't make a change until you can easily complete two sets at the advanced level using weight. And remember, whenever you add weight, go back to the intermediate level and work up to the advanced level again.

122   You do this exercise standing up. If you have a bad back, you can sit on a straight-backed chair, using your legs for support.

- Check for proper body alignment: feet shoulder width, knees slightly flexed, abdominals in, shoulders back, chest up, head in neutral position.

- Grasp the weights firmly (don't squeeze them).

- Raise your elbows to shoulder height as shown in pictures A and B.

- Now, raise your arms slightly as shown in pictures C and D. This is a very short movement. I want the work to come from your shoulders, not your arms. Concentrate. Think about isolating the muscle group you are trying to change.

- Return to the starting position and repeat.

A

B

C

D

Exercise #16

●

SHOULDER SIDE RAISES

This exercise is for your shoulder muscles (deltoids). It will help build up your shoulders, giving your torso flare and taper. Women (and some men) will find that they may no longer need shoulder pads. Shoulder side raises will make men's shoulders bigger and wider and will give women a nice shape and a dynamite new look in strapless dresses.

After you perfect your technique you'll need hand weights for this exercise:

- Women should begin with three to five pounds; men with ten to fifteen pounds.

- Check to make sure your body is properly aligned: feet shoulder width apart, knees flexed, abdominals pulled in and buttocks contracted to protect your back, head in neutral position, eyes front.

- Grasp your weights firmly (don't squeeze them). Your arms should be slightly rounded as shown in picture A.

- Raise and squeeze your arms to shoulder level (*no higher*) as shown in picture B. Make sure your palms are facing the floor.

- Do *not* swing your arms. Feel the effort in your shoulders. Lower your arms slowly and smoothly. Don't just drop them. *Control* the movement so that you raise and lower your arms at the same pace. You should feel the effort in your shoulders.

Eventually men can add weight and do low repetitions (eight to ten) to build bulk. Women want contour, which you get from higher reps (fifteen or more) with less weight.

A

B

Exercise #17

●

SHOULDER FRONTAL RAISES

This exercise adds to the effects of shoulder side raises. You do them exactly the same way except instead of raising your arms to the sides, you raise them to the front. The model in picture A demonstrates proper starting position. Emphasis of this movement is for more front deltoid development.

- Check for proper body alignment: shoulder width stance, knees flexed, abs in, chest up, head in neutral position.

- Grasp your weight firmly, without squeezing. Your arms should be slightly rounded.

- Raise your arms out in front of you one at a time as the model is doing in picture B—only as high or slightly higher than your shoulders. Squeeze your muscles.

- Return to the starting position. Concentrate on the movement. Control the weight, and lift and lower your arms slowly and smoothly. Don't jerk them up or drop them down. Think about the muscles you're working. *feel them when you work them.*

A

B

Exercise #18

●

TRICEPS EXTENSIONS

This exercise, also called the overhead triceps press, tones and strengthens the triceps muscles (**triceps brachii**) in the back of the upper arm. Firming up these muscles should help eliminate "granny arms" and will give a nice shape and contour to the upper arms. No more jiggly flesh. The triceps make up two-thirds of arm size. A man can increase his total arm size quickly with these exercises.

Do this exercise without weight until you've perfected your technique. Then you'll need one hand weight. Women can use three to five pounds; men can start with ten to fifteen pounds (or more if you want bigger muscles).

- You can do this exercise standing or sitting as the model is doing in picture A. Either way, check for proper body alignment: feet shoulder width apart, knees slightly flexed, abdominals pulled in, chest up, head neutral.

- Grasp the weight in your right hand, raise your right arm above your head, and bend your elbow so that the weight comes down to the back of your neck as shown in picture A.

- Keep your elbow as close to your head as possible. If it moves as you work, the exercise won't be effective for your triceps. The palm of your hand should be parallel to your head.

- Raise the weight above your head as shown in picture B, *squeeze* the muscle, and then lower your arm to the starting position.

Don't jerk your arm up or let it drop. The movement should be smooth and controlled. You can help stabilize your working arm by holding your right triceps with your left hand. This will also enable you to feel the muscle contracting as you raise your arm.

Repeat the exercise for your left arm.

A

B

Alternate Exercise
●
TRICEPS KICKBACK

This is a good triceps exercise to use for variety. (I can't let you get bored!) Use it to replace Exercise #18 or add it to your routine right after triceps extension.

- Stand with your left leg in front of the right by about two feet and your left knee bent. You can also do this exercise by leaning on a chair as shown in picture A or place the palm of your left hand on your left thigh just above the knee for support.

- Tighten your abs and make sure your chest is lifted and your back is straight. Your head should be in neutral position—don't let it drop down during the exercise.

- Bend your right arm at the elbow as shown in picture A.

- Straighten your right arm by squeezing the triceps muscle as shown in picture B. *Feel it.* If you don't, the exercise is a waste of time. This should be a slow, controlled movement. Keep your elbow close to your side and in one fixed position. Don't jerk your arm back.

- Repeat for your left arm.

A

B

KARIN AND HANY GHALY

Brick, New Jersey

Karin and Hany decided to get into shape together, and they did a fabulous job in just five months on my workout program. Karin lost seventeen pounds and dropped from a size 14 to a size 10. But she says Hany is the real success story: he lost fifty-one pounds and ten pants' sizes!

"We've been married seven years, and Hany has never looked better," Karin wrote.

Hany made the incredible change in his body by working out along with one of my videotapes, following my stepper program, and eating a low-fat diet. "I never want to see that fat guy again," he says of his former self.

Hany and Karin say they've never gotten bored with the exercise plan. "Hany loves competing against you," Karin told me. "In fact, he wants to know when you're going to release a new, more challenging program."

The Ghalys are happier and healthier than ever, and they're thrilled with their great **133** new bodies. They should be. They've done a terrific job because they believe in themselves!

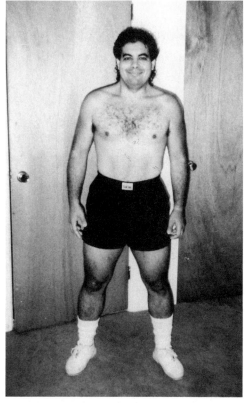

Exercise #19
●
ALTERNATING BICEP CURLS

Everybody knows the biceps, the muscles in the front of the upper arm, the ones you show off when you "make a muscle" with your arm. This exercise will build up your biceps. Eventually men can gain bulk and strength by using heavier and heavier weights (as long as technique is perfect—never sacrifice technique to work with heavier weight). Women will get better contour with lighter weights and higher repetitions.

You'll use hand weights for your biceps curls. Women can begin with three to five pounds; men can use ten to fifteen pounds.

- Check for proper body alignment: feet shoulder width apart, knees flexed, abdominals pulled in, chest up, shoulders back, head in neutral position.

- Grasp a weight in each hand. Your elbows should be close to your body, as if they were resting on the top of your pelvic bone, as shown in picture A.

- Raise and lower first your right arm and then your left, bringing the weight up to your shoulders as shown in picture B. *Squeeze* the muscle to raise your arm. Don't let your elbow move away from your body. Concentrate on what you're doing. You will not get results if you just go through the motions.

- If you turn your palm out as the model is doing in the picture, you'll get better range of motion to give your biceps more work. (The correct terminology for turning the palm out is **supination.**)

- Exhale as you raise your arm; inhale as you lower it. If that's awkward for you, just breathe normally.

- Don't swing your arms up and down. All the work should come from the biceps. Concentrate on the muscle. *Squeeze* your biceps, then lower slowly. Feel the movement.

A

B

C

You can do this exercise sitting down. The technique is the same. Be sure your body is properly aligned.

Alternate Bicep Exercise
●
CONCENTRATION CURLS

Use this exercise to replace Exercise #19, or add it to your routine for more results. You can do concentration curls sitting down.

- Bend forward slightly (make sure your abs are in and your back is straight and strong).

- Lean your left hand on your left thigh. This creates a stronger foundation and allows you to get the most work out of your bicep. Keep tight all over when doing this exercise.

- Hold a dumbbell in your right hand. Rest your elbow against your leg for support as shown in picture A. Next, curl your arm up to your chest as shown in the picture. Keep the palm of your hand curling parallel to your bicep throughout the up and down movement. Do this slowly. Concentrate on your bicep. *Squeeze* the muscle. Lower your arm slowly.

- Repeat for your left arm.

A

B

Exercise #20

●

ZOTTMAN CURLS

This is an exercise for muscles in your forearm. Zottman curls may look like biceps curls, but don't be fooled. Look at the hand position of the model in picture A. His palms aren't turned up or down, they're facing his body.

- Check for proper body alignment: feet shoulder width apart, knees flexed, abs pulled in, chest up, shoulders back, and head in neutral position.

- Add weight only after you've perfected your technique. Grasp dumbbells in each hand (three to five pounds or less for women, ten to fifteen pounds for men). Make sure your palms are facing your body.

- Stand with your arms at your sides as shown in picture A.

- Bend your elbow and raise your arm slowly as shown in picture B. *Squeeze* as you raise your arms. *Squeeze* as you lower them slowly to the starting position. Repeat for your other arm.

A

B

COOLDOWN

- Shake out your arms. This should be an easy, loose movement.

- Walk around, kicking out your feet. Just wander around the room or even around the house.

- Round your arms and stretch them gently in front of your chest as if you were about to hug yourself.

- Now, repeat the stretches on pages 100–109 to help your muscles recover and prevent soreness.

Congratulate yourself. You're well on the way to a fantastic, strong, shapely body. That's it for today. Next week we add aerobics to your workout. You'll be ready. You already are a lot stronger than you were two weeks ago. And you'll be even stronger two weeks from now.

You're kicking butt now!

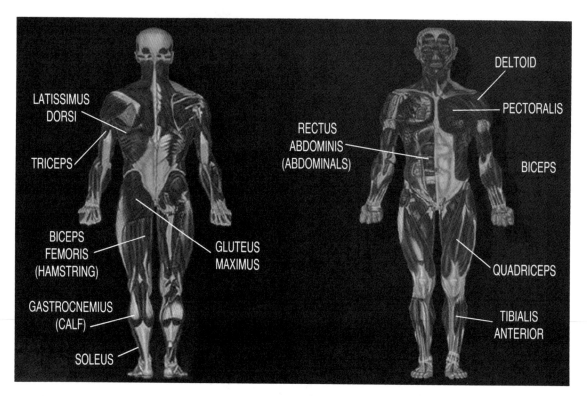

You're now working on all the major muscles of your body!

WEEK THREE:
TOTAL BODY REJUVENATION WORKOUT

This is your third week into the Total Body Rejuvenation program. Start with your active warm-up and static stretching as usual. Then do the upper body stretches I've added to your *killer* routine.

Exercise for the muscles of the upper body will now be included to finish your Total Body Program, working in order from the largest to the smallest muscle groups: legs, back, chest, shoulders, triceps, biceps, and then forearms.

Again, we'll be concentrating on progressive resistance exercises to tone, firm, shape, and strengthen your physique to your own personal goals.

Note: Upper body week three will be worked every other day with lower body, alternating with the days that you're working abdominal and back exercises.

ABDOMINAL EXERCISES:
  1. Abdominal Curls
  2. Reverse Torso Curls
  3. Oblique Curls
BACK EXERCISES:
  4. Back Extensions
LOWER BODY EXERCISES:
  5. Modified Squats
  6. Wide Stance Squats
  7. Lunges (right and left)
  8. Hip Abduction
  9. Hip Adduction
  10. Heel Raises
  11. Alternate Toe Raises

UPPER BODY EXERCISES:
  12. Back Rows
  13. Chest Presses
  14. Chest Flyes
  15. Shoulder Presses
  16. Shoulder Side Raises
  17. Shoulder Front Raises
  18. Triceps Extensions
  19. Alternate Biceps Curls
  20. Zottman Curls

Note: Men who want to build muscle and lose fat need to stay in the 8–10 repetitions category with weight resistance that makes it hard to complete the 8–10 reps.
Failure: When technique is no longer perfect and you have to swing to get additional reps.

Beginner 6–8 Repetitions (1 Set)	Intermediate 9–15 Repetitions (1 Set)	Advanced 16–25 Repetitions (2 Sets)

WEEK THREE:
TOTAL BODY REJUVENATION WORKOUT

NOTE: Don't forget your active warmup and static stretching before your workout.

SUNDAY OFF	DATE:				DATE:				DATE:			
	MONDAY Upper Body & Lower Body Workout				**TUESDAY** Abdominal, Back & Aerobic Workout				**WEDNESDAY** Upper Body & Lower Body Workout			
		WEIGHT	REPS	SET(S)		WEIGHT	REPS	SET(S)		WEIGHT	REPS	SET(S)
	Exercise #5 Modified Squats				Exercise #1 Abdominal Curls				Exercise #5 Modified Squats			
	Exercise #6 Wide Stance Squats				Exercise #2 Reverse Torso Curls				Exercise #6 Wide Stance Squats			
	Exercise #7 Lunges (RT & LT)				Exercise #3 Oblique Curls				Exercise #7 Lunges (RT & LT)			
	Exercise #8 Hip Abduction				Exercise #4 Back Extensions				Exercise #8 Hip Abduction			
	Exercise #9 Hip Adduction								Exercise #9 Hip Adduction			
	Exercise #10 Heel Raises								Exercise #10 Heel Raises			
	Exercise #11 Alternate Toe Raises								Exercise #11 Alternate Toe Raises			
	Exercise #12 Back Rows								Exercise #12 Back Rows			
	Exercise #13 Chest Presses								Exercise #13 Chest Presses			
	Exercise #14 Chest Flyes								Exercise #14 Chest Flyes			
	Exercise #15 Shoulder Presses								Exercise #15 Shoulder Presses			
	Exercise #16 Shoulder Side Raises								Exercise #16 Shoulder Side Raises			
	Exercise #17 Shoulder Front Raises								Exercise #17 Shoulder Front Raises			
	Exercise #18 Triceps Extensions								Exercise #18 Triceps Extensions			
	Exercise #19 Alternate Biceps Curls								Exercise #19 Alternate Biceps Curls			
	Exercise #20 Zottman Curls								Exercise #20 Zottman Curls			

WEEK THREE:
TOTAL BODY REJUVENATION WORKOUT

NOTE: Don't forget your active warmup and static stretching before your workout.

DATE:				DATE:				DATE:			
THURSDAY Abdominal, Back & Aerobic Workout				**FRIDAY** Upper Body & Lower Body Workout				**SATURDAY** Abdominal, Back & Aerobic Workout			
	WEIGHT	REPS	SET(S)		WEIGHT	REPS	SET(S)		WEIGHT	REPS	SET(S)
Exercise #1 Abdominal Curls				Exercise #5 Squats				Exercise #1 Abdominal Curls			
Exercise #2 Reverse Torso Curls				Exercise #6 Wide Stance Squats				Exercise #2 Reverse Torso Curls			
Exercise #3 Oblique Curls				Exercise #7 Lunges (RT & LT)				Exercise #3 Oblique Curls			
Exercise #4 Back Extensions				Exercise #8 Hip Abduction				Exercise #4 Back Extensions			
				Exercise #9 Hip Adduction							
				Exercise #10 Heel Raises							
				Exercise #11 Alternate Toe Raises							
				Exercise #12 Back Rows							
				Exercise #13 Chest Presses							
				Exercise #14 Chest Flyes							
				Exercise #15 Shoulder Presses							
				Exercise #16 Shoulder Side Raises							
				Exercise #17 Shoulder Front Raises							
				Exercise #18 Triceps Extensions							
				Exercise #19 Alternate Biceps Curls							
				Exercise #20 Zottman Curls							

6
Week Four:
AEROBIC/CARDIOVASCULAR

Now for something completely different: the fourth and last part of your workout program, aerobic/cardiovascular exercise. This includes outdoor activities like walking, running, biking, and cross-country skiing or working out indoors at home or at a gym on a treadmill, stationary bike, indoor skiing, or stepping machine.

The word *aerobic* means "with air." Your body needs oxygen to perform aerobic exercise. With every breath we inhale oxygen, which is then carried throughout the body via the blood the heart pumps through the circulatory system. The combination of the heart and blood vessels is called the **cardio-** (heart) **vascular** (vessels) system. Aerobic activity also conditions your lungs and respiratory system. To remind you of the important health benefits of this part of your workout, I have referred to it throughout this book as "aerobic/cardiovascular activity."

To understand how aerobic/cardiovascular exercise conditions your heart and lungs, you have to know a bit about your body's needs during vigorous activity. When you're working out, your body demands more oxygen than it normally requires. Since oxygen is extracted from blood, during exercise your heart must pump more blood than it does when your body is at rest. Over time, this increased demand conditions the heart and lungs and improves blood circulation.

FACT: When you're out of shape, it takes your heart seventy to seventy-five beats to pump the same amount of blood it can handle in forty-five to fifty beats when you're physically fit. This means that your heart works at a less efficient rate, using more beats to pump blood when your lifestyle is sedentary. Don't wear your ticker out!

Aerobic/cardiovascular exercise also revs up your metabolism so that your body burns calories and fat at an accelerated rate while you're working out. Even after you stop exercising, your metabolism may not slow down for hours. The faster you burn calories, the faster you lose weight and the more food you can eat without gaining weight once you reach your goal. By adding aerobic/cardiovascular activity to the resistance and flexibility exercises you've been doing for the past three weeks, *you'll burn fat faster.* This is the balance of exercise concepts that is the key to long-lasting, high-energy results.

Here's the deal: In building your lean muscle mass, which shapes the contour of your body, you increase your metabolic rate. Aerobic/cardiovascular exercise draws on fat as its main source of fuel after the first fifteen minutes of activity. Because of its effects on metabolism, you continue to burn calories at a faster pace even after you finish exercising.

Remember, calorie *burning,* not calorie *cutting,* is the key to lasting change.

This combination produces results, and it delivers them faster than any diet possibly can and more efficiently than any workout plan I've seen. Follow it, and you'll soon have a success story of your own. You'll be slim and fit, with a great body and a whole new attitude toward life.

To get the full health and fitness benefits of aerobic/cardiovascular exercise, you have to work out for *at least* twenty minutes a day three times a week. You may not be able to do that much at first. Start at the beginner's level just as you did for your resistance training workout. But from the outset you will be challenging yourself to achieve the results you want. Make every workout longer and more intense than the one before. Every added minute makes a difference.

Your goal is to raise your heart rate high enough to get the full benefits of aerobic/cardiovascular exercise. I'll explain how to determine whether your heart rate is as high as it should be during your workout. When you do aerobic/cardiovascular exercise for at least thirty minutes a day three times a week at your target heart rate, results are guaranteed. And that's a scientific fact.

TARGET HEART RATE

To get the most out of aerobic/cardiovascular exercise, you need to raise your heart rate into the "target zone" appropriate for your age. The target zone is 60 to 85 percent of your maximum heart rate. When you're in your target zone, you know you're working out at the intensity needed to get results. The chart on page 147 shows the maximum heart rate for ages twenty through seventy.

At first your goal should be to get your heart rate into the 60 percent range. That will become easier over time. Your heart will have become more efficient and won't have to work as hard to meet the demands of exercise. Eventually you can aim for the 75 percent range. If you're in really good shape, you can work out at 85 percent of your maximum heart rate. Even for an athlete 85 percent is enough. Don't even think about pushing it farther.

FIND YOUR TARGET ZONE

Age	60–85%	Maximum (100%) Heart Rate
20	120–170 beats per min.	200
25	117–166 beats per min.	195
30	114–162 beats per min.	190
35	111–157 beats per min.	185
40	108–153 beats per min.	180
45	105–149 beats per min.	175
50	102–146 beats per min.	170
55	99–140 beats per min.	165
60	96–136 beats per min.	160
65	93–132 beats per min.	155
70	90–128 beats per min.	150

For a more precise idea of your maximum heart rate and target zone, subtract your age from 220. Multiply your maximum heart rate by .60 and then by .85. Here's an example using my age, thirty-seven:

- $220 - 37 = 183$
- $183 \times .60 = 110$
- $183 \times .85 = 156$

TAKING YOUR PULSE

To find out whether you are exercising in your target zone, take your pulse twice: first as you begin to exert yourself after your warm-up, then again just before your cooldown. You should be able to feel a pulse in the radial artery on the inside of your wrist in line with your thumb or in the carotid artery on either side of the neck below the jaw and to the side of the throat. To count your pulse, use the tips of the index and middle fingers, not your thumb (there's a pulse in the thumb that can confuse your count). You should be able to feel either pulse with gentle pressure. (Don't press too hard on the carotid artery—too much pressure can slow your heart rate; you won't get a true reading and you may get dizzy.)

148 Once you find your pulse, count the beats for ten seconds and then multiply by six. This will give you the number of beats per minute. Compare your result with the target zone for your age in the chart (or with your own calculations). If your count is under the low end of your zone, you're not working hard enough. If it's above the high end of your zone, slow down: you're working too hard.

IS MORE BETTER?

The longer your aerobic/cardiovascular workout, the more calories you burn, but exercising for more than an hour doesn't add substantially to the conditioning effects. It's my belief that time duration with lower intensity is better for long-term fat burning.

OVERDOING IT

When you're working in your target zone, your exercise should be vigorous and sustained. But don't get carried away by the word *vigorous*. Here are the rules for a safe, effective aerobic/cardiovascular workout:

- You should be able to carry on a conversation while exercising. If you can't talk comfortably, you're working too hard. Ease off until you can.
- If you don't feel normal within ten minutes after you finish exercising, you're working too hard. Ease off.
- If you have trouble breathing, feel faint, or feel weak during or after exercising, you're pushing yourself too hard. Ease off!
- If you get "side stitches" (moderate pain in your side), you're working too hard. Ease off.
- *Never* stop an aerobic/cardiovascular workout abruptly. If you do, you'll deliver a huge shock to your system. This is an absolute Tony Little no-no.

PERCEIVED EXERTION

For your aerobic/cardiovascular workout I want you to key your effort to the perceived exertion chart below. Exercising at the intensity I recommend will enable you to continue for the full amount of time for your level. Remember, with an aerobic/cardiovascular workout the payoff comes from the amount of *time* you spend exercising, not how hard you work at it.

It's better to underexercise and do it right.

PERCEIVED EXERTION CHART

0	No effort at all
0.5	Very, very little effort involved
1	Very little effort to perform
2	A little effort to perform
3	Moderate effort involved
4	Somewhat strong effort needed
5	Good strong effort needed
6	Transition level
7	Very strong effort needed
8	Transition level
9	Nearing maximum effort for you
10	Very, very strong exercise level (maximum)

- *Beginner:* Between levels three and four.
- *Intermediate:* Between levels five and six.
- *Advanced:* Levels seven to ten.

150   THE FULL WORKOUT

Adding aerobic/cardiovascular activity to your fitness program means you'll be working out at least five days a week. Here's the game plan:

- Abdominal exercises every other day.
- Upper and lower body workouts three days a week (both workouts on the same day or on alternate days).
- Aerobic/cardiovascular exercise thirty to sixty minutes a day three days a week.

- *Beginner:* Fifteen to twenty minutes of aerobic/cardiovascular exercise three times a week.
- *Intermediate:* At least twenty-five minutes of aerobic/cardiovascular three times a week.
- *Advanced:* At least thirty minutes (and up to sixty minutes) three times a week.

Balance between exercise methods is the secret to achieving a new body fast—and keeping it. And varying the exercises keeps you from getting bored and hitting plateaus.

A HEALTHY HEART

People always ask me if it's dangerous to take up aerobic/cardiovascular exercise, particularly if you're over forty and haven't been active in years. My answer is always the same: *Not* exercising is much more dangerous.

FACT: The American Heart Association and the U.S. Centers for Disease Control now list a sedentary, couch potato lifestyle as a major risk factor for heart disease. That means being inactive is just as bad for your heart as smoking, high cholesterol, or high blood pressure.

Far from being dangerous, becoming more active is good for you. Exercise conditions your heart and lowers the risk of heart disease in two important ways:

- It helps lower blood pressure.

- It can raise high density lipoprotein (HDL), the "good cholesterol" that protects against heart disease.

Even people who have had heart attacks usually are encouraged to exercise in medically supervised programs. Physical activity can reduce the risk of having another heart attack.

DOCTOR KNOWS BEST

It's always a good idea to check with your doctor when beginning a new exercise program, particularly if you're over thirty-five and haven't been active lately. But don't expect the doc to advise against it. Unless you have a medical condition that would make exercising dangerous, he'll probably advise you to take it easy at first and then congratulate you for making such a healthy decision.

Whatever your age, check with your doctor before beginning an exercise program if you have any of the following:

- recently developed chest pain
- breathlessness after mild exertion
- high blood pressure, for which you take medication
- bone, joint, or back problems
- any medical condition that could make unsupervised exercise dangerous

---

EXERCISE ALERT

Stop exercising and call your doctor immediately if you develop any of the symptoms in the list below. They could mean heart trouble.

- Pain or pressure in the mid- or left-chest area, left neck, shoulder, or arm during or just after exercising
- Sudden light-headedness, cold sweat, pallor, or fainting

MORE REWARDS OF AEROBIC/CARDIOVASCULAR EXERCISE

- Reduces stress
- Increases energy and stamina
- Improves your self-image
- Improves your sleep
- Helps control appetite
- Lessens anxiety
- Relieves depression
- Improves digestion
- Relieves constipation
- Improves your sense of well-being
- Again, and back by popular demand: fat burning

PROTECTING YOUR BONES

Did you know almost any weight-bearing exercise is good for your bones as well as your heart and general mental and physical health? It can help protect against osteoporosis, the bone-thinning disease that leads to millions of hip and spinal fractures among older people.

The best time to worry about your bones is *now!* The younger you are, the better. The more years you spend exercising properly, the stronger your bones will be later in life when they begin to thin and the better you'll be able to withstand the changes that come with age.

After thirty-five both men and women begin losing bone density very slowly. Women have much more to worry about than men because their bones are smaller to start with and after menopause, when levels of the female hormone estrogen fall, women lose bone at a much faster rate than men *ever* do. Without estrogen women's bones are less able to absorb the bone-building mineral calcium.

FACT: Bone, like muscle, is living tissue. Scientific studies have shown that the more exercise you get, the stronger your bones are likely to be.

For strong bones you also have to make sure you get enough calcium in your diet. Calcium needs are discussed in chapter 9. After menopause, women may be advised to take estrogen replacement to protect against osteoporosis.

The best physical activities for bones are weight-bearing aerobic/cardiovascular and strengthening exercises that you do *on your feet!* You can get a great cardiovascular workout from swimming and bicycling (they also contribute to general fitness and calorie burning), but they don't do anything for bones. So stand up and *move!* Walk, jog, hit that treadmill, hop on that stepping machine. *Move* for your bones. Keep them strong. They're the foundation for that dynamite body you're building.

CROSS-TRAINING

On your Total Body Rejuvenation program I want you to do more than one type of aerobic/cardiovascular activity. This is called cross-training, and there are important reasons to switch from one type of activity to another:

1. Physiologically our bodies adapt to the same exercises, hit a plateau, and no longer change in response to what we're doing.
2. Sooner or later we all get bored with the same routine, and we no longer have fun. We must always be challenging ourselves.

Switching from one type of aerobic/cardiovascular activity to another keeps you interested, forces your body to change and keeps your mind "jazzed" about your workouts.

THE IMPACT QUESTION

Most of the aerobic/cardiovascular exercises I recommend are low-impact or nonimpact. You don't have to jump around and risk injury to your bones, joints, and back. But don't be fooled. Low-impact/nonimpact aerobic/cardiovascular exercise is every bit as intense and effective as a high-impact workout like running or aerobic dancing. It's all in the technique.

DRINK WATER!

Always be sure to drink plenty of water before and after an aerobic/cardiovascular or strength training workout to replace fluids lost when you sweat. Your body's most plentiful element is water. Every single body process requires water. The more you drink, the better. Water helps your body flush out toxins. One of the healthiest habits you can form is to drink water, water, water. Sodas and other beverages contain many things besides water. Water is number one.

BLAKE BURI

Colfax, Washington

Can you believe both those pictures are of the same guy? Blake Buri's story is astounding. He weighed 380 pounds as recently as March 1993. That was when he decided the time had come to do something about his body. His "before" picture was taken about the time he began to make the changes that transformed him. The "after" picture was taken at a wedding he attended just eight months later, in December 1993! He lost a grand total of 186 pounds and pared twenty-four inches (that's two *feet!*) from his midsection.

You are what you visualize!

Blake concentrated on my stomach reduction workout for the first three and a half months of his exercise program. Then he bought my cross-country skiing machine. He did his stomach reduction workout in the morning and his aerobic/cardiovascular on the skier at night.

How's that for success? Blake Buri is living proof that my program gets results and gets them fast. Blake believed in himself and went for it.

WHAT ABOUT SPORTS?

I'll bet you are wondering whether you can substitute sports for the aerobic/cardiovascular activities I recommend.

The short answer to that qustion is: No.

Some sports can help you get in shape. But they don't do the job as effectively as sustained vigorous exercise. Even singles tennis, a very fast, very demanding game, entails some standing-around time. For maximum benefit, aerobic/cardiovascular exercise must continue at an intense pace for twenty minutes or longer. The chart on page 157 ranks various activities on the basis of their aerobic/cardiovascular effect. On page 157 you'll find a chart of the calorie-burning effects of different types of aerobic/cardiovascular exercise.

FACT: Walking burns about the same number of calories per mile as running. Walking one mile at a brisk pace takes about fifteen minutes and burns as many calories as jogging a mile in eight and a half minutes.

More good news: If you're heavy, you'll burn more calories walking a mile than a thin person will running a mile. So don't get the idea that low-impact exercise is for wimps. It delivers results, dependably, safely, and consistently.

Because of my back problems, I'm definitely prejudiced in favor of low-impact/nonimpact aerobic/cardiovascular exercise. If you haven't been active recently, I *insist* that you stick to a low-impact/nonimpact aerobic/cardiovascular program until you get in shape. You can't run a marathon if the most exercise you've been doing lately is strolling through the supermarket aisles. Build your aerobic capacity gradually. You'll be surprised at how quickly you improve if you follow this program.

AEROBIC EFFECTS OF ACTIVITIES

Most Effective

Aerobic dancing
Bicycling
Cross-country skiing
Hiking (uphill)
Ice hockey
Jogging
Jumping rope
Rowing
Running in place
Stair climbing
Stationary cycling
Swimming
Brisk walking

Moderately Effective

Downhill skiing
Basketball
Field hockey
Calisthenics
Handball
Racquetball
Soccer
Squash
Tennis (singles)
Volleyball
Walking moderately

Ineffective

Badminton
Baseball
Bowling
Croquet
Football
Gardening
Golf
Housework
Ping-Pong
Shuffleboard
Social dancing
Softball

Source: *Exercise and Your Heart*, National Heart, Lung, and Blood Institute.

BURNING CALORIES

Activity	Calories burned*
Bicycling, 6 mph	240 cals./hr.
Bicycling, 12 mph	410 cals./hr.
Cross-country skiing	700 cals./hr.
Jogging, 5½ mph	740 cals./hr.
Jogging, 7 mph	920 cals./hr.
Jumping rope	750 cals./hr.
Running in place	650 cals./hr.
Swimming, 25 yds./min.	275 cals./hr.
Swimming, 50 yds./min.	500 cals./hr.
Tennis, singles	400 cals./hr.
Walking, 2 mph	240 cals./hr.
Walking, 3 mph	320 cals./hr.
Walking, 4½ mph	440 cals./hr.

*By a 150-pound person. A 100-pound person would burn one-third fewer calories and a 200-pound person, one-third more calories.

Source: *Exercise and Your Heart*, National Heart, Lung, and Blood Institute.

158   WARMING UP AND COOLING DOWN

A warm-up, static stretching, and cooldown are just as important in an aerobic/cardio-vascular workout as they are in resistance exercise training. You don't have to do anything special to warm up or cool down. Just begin your workout at an easy pace and increase your speed gradually over three to five minutes. The principle here is the same as it is in your resistance workout: If you don't warm up your muscles, they'll be more prone to injury.

To cool down after an aerobic/cardiovascular workout, just slow your pace and continue moving until your heart rate comes back to normal. Remember, if you stop exercising abruptly when you're in your target zone, you could get dizzy. More important, it's a shock to your heart. This is a Tony Little absolute *no-no*.

Bear these basics in mind as you read through the sections ahead on specific types of aerobic/cardiovascular exercise. I'll keep reminding you to warm up and cool down.

STATIC STRETCHING

You already have learned the stretches below as part of your resistance workout. The following combination will better prepare you for any of the aerobic/cardiovascular workouts described in the pages ahead. If you need to be reminded of what these stretches look like, just refer to the lower body and upper body workout chapters.

Hold each stretch for ten counts until you get a comfortable stretching sensation, not a painful one. Don't force it!

- *Low back stretch:* Lie on your back. Bend your knees into your chest and pull them in gently. Picture number one.
- *Alternate leg low back stretch:* Lie on your back with both legs stretched out. Bend your right knee and put your right foot flat on the floor. Raise your left leg straight up. Keeping your knee slightly flexed, gently pull your leg in toward your chest. Repeat for your right leg. Picture number two.
- *Lateral low back and quadriceps stretch:* Lie on your right side. Bend your left leg and stretch it toward the floor. At the same time stretch your left arm out on the floor in the opposite direction. Repeat for the other side. Picture number three.
- *Back extension:* Lying on your stomach, push your chest up with your arms. Picture number four.
- *Full back and hip stretch:* Sit back toward your heels and stretch your upper body and arms out on the floor in front of you. Picture number five.
- *Seated calf stretch:* Sit up straight on the floor with your legs extended in front of you. Flex your feet until you feel a stretch in your calves. Picture number six.
- *Lunge stretch:* Kneel on the floor with your right leg bent at the knee and your right foot flat on the floor. Lean into your right leg. Repeat for the left leg. Picture number seven.

- *Calf stretch:* Standing up, take a wide stance, your right leg in front of the left. Keeping your left heel flat on the floor and your right knee slightly bent, lean into your right leg until you feel a stretch in your left calf. Repeat for the other leg. Picture number eight.
- *Shoulder stretch:* Standing up, stretch your right arm across your chest and push it in toward the chest with your left hand. Repeat for the left side. Picture number nine.
- *Shrugs:* Loosen up by shrugging and rolling your shoulders three times. Picture number ten.
- *Front and posterior neck stretch:* Look down toward the floor to get a stretch in the back of your neck. Look up toward the ceiling to get a stretch in the front. *Don't force* either of these stretches beyond what is comfortable.
- *Lateral neck stretch:* Lean your head toward your right shoulder. Repeat, leaning your head toward your left shoulder. *Don't force* this stretch.

See the photos on pages 65 to 71 to help remind you of what these stretching exercises look like.

ALL ABOUT WALKING

Sure you know how to walk. Who doesn't? But do you know how to turn walking into a great workout? Did you know that the more overweight and out of shape you are, the more effective a walking program can be?

If you're new to aerobic/cardiovascular exercise, walking is the way to start. After all, every day you walk somewhere—even if it's just to the refrigerator. And you don't need any special equipment other than a good pair of comfortable shoes.

Choosing Shoes

If you don't have the right shoes, you're not going to be happy walking. Who wants sore feet as a reward for exercise? And let's face it, if your feet start to hurt while you're walking, you can't keep up the brisk pace needed for an effective workout. You can use cross-training shoes or good walking shoes. Here's a checklist to use when shopping for shoes:

- Are they comfortable?
- Do they provide good support?
- Do they have arch supports?
- Is the heel at least half an inch higher than the sole?
- Is the upper part made of leather, nylon mesh, or other material that can breathe?
- Go to a reputable shoe store and ask for the shoes that would best match your program.

The Right Route

The great thing about walking is that you can do it any time, anywhere. Just open the door and go. If you can't schedule your workout until after dark and you aren't comfortable walking out of doors at night, try a shopping mall. Many malls open early and stay open late to accommodate people who want to walk indoors.

When choosing an outdoor route, look for a soft, smooth surface. A running track at a nearby high school or college is ideal.

It's harder to keep up a brisk pace if you're walking on crowded city sidewalks or in busy areas where you have to stop frequently to wait for traffic lights to change and breathe in carbon monoxide. You would be better off walking in a park or quiet residential area—even if you have to drive to get there. (I personally prefer a high quality motorized treadmill over any other type of aerobic equipment and outdoor walking.)

Safety First

- If you exercise at dusk or after dark, wear light-colored clothing with a reflecting band so that drivers can spot you easily. This also applies during bad weather.
- Walk toward oncoming traffic, and don't assume drivers will see you.

Cold-Weather Tips

- Dress in layers so you can peel some off if you get too warm.
- Wear gloves.
- Wear a hat: up to 40 percent of body heat is lost through the neck and head.
- Avoid outdoor exercise in icy conditions.

Hot-Weather Tips

- Work out early or late—not in the heat of the sun.
- Drink lots of water before, during, and after your workout.
- Dress lightly in loose-fitting clothing.
- Don't wear plastic suits, sweatshirts, or sweatpants. They'll make you sweat more, but you won't lose weight any faster—you'll just replace the lost fluids as soon as you start to drink again. This kind of workout gear can also contribute to high temperatures and, possibly, heat stroke.

WARNING: There are some days when you should *never* exercise out of doors. They are the "Black Flag" days when the air temperature is over 100 degrees Fahrenheit and the relative humidity is 100 percent. It's also dangerous to exercise out of doors when the air temperature exceeds 85 degrees Fahrenheit and the relative humidity is over 90 percent.

Warm-Weather Alert

Don't neglect signs of heat exhaustion and heat stroke when walking, jogging, or running outdoors in hot weather. Be sure to drink enough liquids to replace fluids lost during exercise. If symptoms occur, stop what you're doing, get out of the heat, drink cool liquids, and cool your body down with wet towels.

Heat exhaustion

Heavy sweating
Headache
Nausea and vomiting
Confusion
Body temperature to fall below normal

Heat stroke

Dizziness
Headache
Nausea
Thirst
Muscle cramps
*The body to stop sweating suddenly
*High body temperature

*This could be dangerous. Get medical help immediately.

Technique

Proper technique is just as important in walking as an aerobic/cardiovascular activity as it is in resistance training. Start out right:

- Keep your knees slightly flexed.
- Pull in your abdominal muscles.
- Hold your chest up.
- Keep your back slightly retracted.
- Hold your head in neutral position.

How Long, How Far?

- *Beginner:*
    1. *Warm-up*: Five minutes at an easy pace
    2. *Workout*: Walk briskly for up to ten minutes
    3. *Cooldown*: Five minutes at an easy pace
- *Intermediate:*
    1. *Warmup*: Five minutes at an easy pace
    2. *Workout*: Walk briskly for up to twenty minutes
    3. *Cooldown*: Five minutes at an easy pace
- *Advanced:*
    1. *Warmup*: Five minutes at an easy pace
    2. *Workout*: Walk briskly for up to sixty minutes
    3. *Cooldown*: Five minutes at an easy pace

Don't forget: Your goal is to exercise *in your target heart rate zone.* Take your pulse just before you start your cooldown. If your heart rate is *below* your target zone, work harder next time. If it's *above* the target zone, take it easy. You're working too hard.

JOGGING

Jogging is a high-impact exercise, so if you've had back problems or joint injuries, you probably will be better off sticking with a low-impact workout. And if you're out of shape, you definitely should approach jogging gradually, only after building up your stamina with walking or another aerobic workout. Regardless of your age, I would rather you get a doctor's okay before you begin to jog. And you better have high performance shoes.

Wrong Way

Right Way

THE WALK TEST

This excellent test of readiness for running comes from the President's Council on Physical Fitness and Sports. I suggest you use it to judge your readiness for jogging.

The test: It's okay to start jogging if you can comfortably walk three miles in forty-five minutes.

All of the precautions suggested in the walking section apply to jogging. Be very choosy about foot support: you'll need special running shoes, since the pair you used for walking aren't necessarily the best for jogging. Every year the running magazines rate all of the major brands on the market, so it may be worth a trip to the library to see what's recommended.

Getting Started

Technique matters in jogging, too. But in addition to the basic body position you must maintain for all forms of exercise, you need to learn correct jogging technique. Check the illustrations above for the right and wrong ways to jog.

- Keep your back straight and your head up. Don't let yourself lean forward excessively.
- Carry your arms slightly away from your body with your elbows bent so that your forearms are roughly parallel to the ground.
- Land on your heels and roll forward on your foot to push yourself off. Your legs will get sore if you jog on the balls of your feet.
- Keep your stride relatively short—don't reach for distance.
- Breathe deeply with your mouth open.

The Workout

- *Stretching:* Do the static stretches on pages 158–159 both before and *after* the jog.
- *Warming Up:* Unlike other aerobic/cardiovascular activities, you don't warm up for jogging by jogging. Instead spend the the first five minutes walking or walking in place, circling your arms, and lifting one knee and then the other toward your chest.
- *Cooling Down:* Slow your pace from a jog to a brisk walk and then to an easy walking pace or walking in place. Don't stop moving until your heart rate slow almost back to your starting heart rate.
- *Stretching:* Repeat the stretches on pages 158–159.

WORKING OUT INDOORS

You can do your aerobic/cardiovascular workout at home, at a gym, or at a health club. If you decide to work out at home, you'll need to invest in some equipment: a stationary or recumbent bike, skiing machine, treadmill, or stepping machine. (For information on my line of home fitness equipment, please see appendix 3.) Most gyms have bikes, treadmills, and stair-stepping machines, and many also offer aerobic exercise classes.

STATIONARY/RECUMBENT BICYCLING

You know what a stationary bike looks like, but you may not be familiar with a recumbent bike. The principal difference is the seat. A stationary bike has a typical saddle seat, while a recumbent bike has a wide, cushioned comfortable seat with back support. Recumbent bikes distribute your weight evenly. You won't get sore from perching on a tiny seat. I definitely recommend a recumbent bike if you have back problems. Recumbent bikes also give you better aerobic benefits because they position your body so your knees are higher than your heart. As an extra added attraction, they work your hip, buttock, and thigh muscles better than a regular stationary bike.

If you're very overweight, a recumbent bike or treadmill should be your first choice for an aerobic/cardiovascular workout.

Adjusting the Bike

When you work out on a bike (either kind), you must position the seat for comfort and so that your legs are slightly flexed when you're in the "down" position.

If you work out on a bike at a gym or health club, you also may have to adjust the handlebars so that you can reach them easily while keeping your back straight. If you have to lean down or stretch to hold on, you won't have a comfortable workout and

166 you could hurt your back. At a gym, ask a trainer to help you find the best position for you. Make a note of the seat and handlebar positions so that you can adjust the bike, if necessary, for each workout.

Buying a Bike

The advantage of buying your own bike is that you can work out at home at your convenience. If you decide to buy, look for the following features:

- A two-year warranty (minimum)
- A seat low enough to accommodate proper body alignment
- Smooth and quiet movement

Computer features and other bells and whistles may make a bike appealing to you, but they're not as important as the structural integrity and quality of movement of the unit.

A bike is an important investment. It's sometimes worth spending some extra money for better equipment that will last and be used for a longer period of time.

Some bikes have movable handlebars, a "dual action" feature you can use for upper body exercise while you work out. Don't use the dual action features as a beginner. At the intermediate or advanced levels you can burn more calories and get a more effective workout if a bike has the additional capability. When you hold the handlebars with an overhand grip, you work your triceps, shoulder, chest, and abdominal muscles. With an underhand grip, you work your biceps and "lats" (back muscles).

Also look for a bike that comes with an instructional and motivational video. If you can't find one, call my office for help.

The Workout

Whichever bike you choose, the workout is the same:

1. *Static stretch* (see pages 158–159)
2. *Warm-up* (see page 164)
3. *Workout and cooldown*
   - *Beginner:* Ten minutes + two-minute or more cooldown
   - *Intermediate:* Twenty minutes (include one thirty-second sprint and one sixty-second sprint) + three-minute or more cooldown
   - *Advanced:* Thirty minutes (include one thirty-second sprint, two sixty-second sprints, and one ninety-second sprint) + four-minute or more cooldown

All levels: Don't get off the bike until your heart rate comes down to 110–120 beats per minute. After you get off the bike, spend five more minutes cooling down: walk around, shake out your legs. Loosen up.

STEPPING MACHINE

Not only do stepping machines give you a great aerobic workout, they go a long way to cure the droopy buttock syndrome. For leg and buttock shaping, stepping machines can't be beat. They also are powerful fat burners on a par with running.

You can use stepping machines at a gym or health club or buy one for home use. If you work out at a gym, ask a trainer to go over the features of the machine and explain how to use it. You can adjust most machines to vary the intensity of your workout. Ask the trainer how to set the machine for a beginning level with low resistance. Don't increase resistance until you can comfortably complete a thirty-two-minute advanced workout.

Many of the stepping machines in gyms and health clubs let you set the time you plan to work and then turn themselves off when your time is up. Some give you a readout of the calories burned, the "flights" climbed, and your number of steps per minute.

A stepping machine for home use should include the following features. Take a look at the one shown at the chapter opening.

- wide foot pedals
- a wide, sturdy base that doesn't rock
- easy, simple, and quiet movement
- two-year warranty (minimum)

Be sure to stand on the unit to see if your knees go out past your toes as you step. If this does happen, look for another stepper.

Some stepping machines have a capacity similar to the dual action feature of stationary and recumbent bikes to give upper body exercise along with your aerobic/cardiovascular workout. You don't have to use both features, but it's nice to have the choice.

DAN BURNS

Mercer, Pennsylvania

"**C**ount me as one of your successes," wrote Dan Burns in October 1993.

I can't improve upon his amazing story, so I'll let him tell it in his own words:

"Believe it or not (and I still can't believe it!) I started your exercise program on May 1, 1993, and five months and twenty-two days later I had lost 118 pounds. I lost twenty inches off my waist and went from wearing a 4X shirt and size 56 pants to a 'large' shirt and size 36 pants.

"The only diet I used was low-fat foods. I did the resistance training workout every other day and rode a bike, walked, or swam on the alternate days.

"Now working out is part of my daily routine. It seems to keep up my energy and keep off the weight.

"Tony, you totally changed my life. I'll *never* be out of shape again."

The Workout

Think *technique* before you get on the stepper. As you work out, your knees should be slightly flexed, your abdominals in, your chest up, and your head in a neutral position.

To begin, all you have to do is get on the stepper and press and release the pedals. Don't let the pedals go all the way down or come all the way up. And make sure your knees are not out over your toes.

In general, the more range of motion in your steps, the harder the workout.

- *Beginner:* Take short steps only.
- *Intermediate:* Take short and medium steps. Medium steps will work your thighs (quadriceps) and buttocks (gluteus maximus).
- *Advanced:* Take short, medium, and deep steps. The deeper your step (without letting the pedal hit bottom), the greater your range of motion and the more muscle toning you get.

1. *Static stretch* (see pages 158–159)
2. *Warm-up* (five to ten minutes at an easy pace)
3. *Workout and cooldown*
   - *Beginner:* Ten minutes + two-minute (or more) cooldown
   - *Intermediate:* Twenty minutes + three-minute (or more) cooldown
   - *Advanced:* Thirty-two to forty-five minutes + five-minute cooldown

TREADMILL

This is my ultimate choice for in-home cardiovascular workouts. You can get the same intense workout on a treadmill as you can by walking or jogging out of doors. The advantage is that you can exercise on a treadmill year-round regardless of the weather. And since some treadmills come equipped with an upper body exercise capability, you can work your arms or chest while you're walking.

Almost all gyms and health clubs are equipped with treadmills, and they've also become a popular piece of home exercise equipment. If you work out at a gym or health club, ask one of the trainers to demonstrate how the treadmill works and show you how to use it. If you want to buy a treadmill for home use, look for one with the following features:

- a wide, long base
- a two-horsepower (or more) motor
- adjustable elevation (preferably electronic)
- good-quality low-impact walking surface, preferably with a cushion under the belt or some other type of impact reduction system.
- a cut-off switch to attach to your clothing that turns the machine off if you lose your balance.
- good computer readout
- minimum 2-year warranty
- a Personal Trainer™ video to educate and motivate you.

Clothing

You can use cross-trainers or walking shoes for a treadmill workout. But don't wear running shoes unless jogging or running because the heel is too wide to permit proper walking movement.

You'll also need some good socks that won't bunch up or wrinkle as cotton socks tend to do when they soak up sweat. Look for socks made with a synthetic material that have good padding, wick moisture off your feet, and stay smooth.

If you wear shorts while exercising, make sure that they're loose fitting and comfortable so that they don't chafe the insides of your legs (cotton lycra biker pants are good for this). Your shirt should also be loose fitting enough to allow your arms full range of motion.

> **TIP:** If you are very heavy and your thighs rub together when you walk, apply some petroleum jelly to the insides of your thighs. This will prevent chafing and enable you to exercise comfortably.

Technique

Proper body alignment is key to an effective treadmill workout. Check yourself before you begin:

- Knees flexed.
- Abs in.
- Chest up, back retracted.
- Head in neutral position.

Your stride should be natural. Don't exaggerate your movement or lengthen your normal stride.

As you walk, your heel should come down first. Push off from the toes of your back foot.

Don't tense your shoulders as you walk. Your arms should swing naturally at your sides. Don't let your arms cross your trunk as you walk.

> **TIP:** Until you get comfortable with the treadmill, hold on to the handles. Stand up straight as you walk. Don't lean forward or support yourself with the handles.

The Workout

This is the longest aerobic workout in the book, but it's not effective. However, because it's less strenuous at first, even beginners can handle a slightly longer program.

1. *Warm-up* (Five to ten minutes; set the treadmill at a slow speed—1.5 to 2 miles per hour)
2. *Static stretch:* (see pages 158–159)
3. *Workout and cooldown*

- *Beginner:* Fifteen to twenty minutes + a three to five minute cooldown
- *Intermediate:* Thirty minutes + a three to five minute cooldown
- *Advanced:* Fifty minutes or more + a five-minute cooldown

TIP: At the intermediate and advanced levels you can make a treadmill workout more interesting and fun by speeding up periodically. Intermediates can do up to three one-minute sprints. Just increase the speed so you have to walk faster. At the advanced level, add three three-minute jogging sprints.

Don't get off the treadmill for two to four minutes (depending on your level). When you do dismount, spend another five minutes walking slowly around the house. Continue moving until your heart rate is down to less than 120 beats per minute.

SKIING MACHINE

Cross-country skiing burns more calories per hour than any other form of aerobic/cardiovascular exercise. It's a fantastic, invigorating workout when you can do it outdoors in the snow. But since you can't depend on the weather to cooperate, you have to do it indoors on a machine. These devices have ski poles and foot pedals that slide back and forth on a track as you stand on them and pretend to ski.

A skiing machine for home use should include the following features:

- a strong, sturdy base
- wide, treaded foot pedals
- simple, smooth gliding movement
- adjustable resistance poles and pedals
- sturdy poles
- almost completely assembled
- minimum two-year warranty
- a Personal Trainer™ video to educate and motivate you

Clothing

A skiing machine workout has a big advantage over cross-country skiing in the snow: you don't have to wear layers and layers of clothes. All you need is cross-training shoes and loose-fitting shorts and top. Don't wear shorts that bind (and could chafe) your legs or limit your range of motion.

Technique

Correct movement on a ski machine is smooth and synchronized, just like real cross-country skiing. The picture shown above illustrates the correct movement: note that when the leg is forward, the arm on the same side of the body is back.

A ski machine workout becomes progressively more difficult with the length of the strides you take. Short strides are easiest and give you an aerobic/cardiovascular workout without doing much for your lower body muscles. A medium stride begins drawing on the inner and outer thigh muscles, the hips, the lower abdomen, and the buttocks. A full stride gives you a good lower body workout.

Beginners take only small strides. At the intermediate level you can add a medium stride, and when you reach the advanced level, you can go to a full stride.

Music as a motivator is extremely important in this exercise.

RULE: Because a ski machine takes some getting used to, *everyone* (regardless of fitness level) should start at the beginner's level. Once you're comfortable on the machine, you can move up to the intermediate and advanced levels as soon as the beginner level becomes too easy.

The Workout

1. *Warm-up* (Five to ten minutes)
2. *Static stretching* (see pages 158–159)
3. *Workout and cooldown*
   - *Beginner:* Ten minutes + a two-minute cooldown *on the machine*
   - *Intermediate:* Twenty minutes + a three-minute or more cooldown *on the machine* (include at least one thirty-second and one sixty-second sprint)
   - *Advanced:* Thirty minutes + a five-minute cooldown *on the machine* (include at least two sixty-second sprints)

After your cooldown on the skier, dismount and walk around. Keep moving until your heart rate drops below 120 beats per minute.

AEROBIC CLASSES

If you're a social animal or don't want to invest in home exercise equipment, you might enjoy working out with others in aerobic classes at gyms or health clubs. At the better places, you're going to see lots of great bodies. Working out with people who are serious about keeping in shape can inspire or depress you. If you've got a competitive streak, you may be strongly motivated by the surroundings and the dedication of others who work hard to get in shape or stay that way.

But if you're embarrassed to be seen in your workout clothes and are something of a klutz (as I am), you probably won't last long. And you may become so discouraged that you give up on exercise entirely, at least for a while.

Still, a good aerobic class provides an excellent workout. Make sure the instructor is well trained and cautious; also make sure that the class is not too advanced for you and that it includes the elements of the workouts described in this chapter:

- an active warm-up of five minutes or more
- static stretching
- a workout lasting thirty minutes or more
- a five- to ten-minute cooldown

TIP: You can't judge an aerobic class by watching. They all look much easier than they are. Even the low-impact classes can be very fast and very advanced. Try at least one class before joining a club or gym. Make sure the tempo of the music and the pace of the class is not too fast for you. And ask plenty of questions before you commit.

CHOOSING A GYM AND/OR A PERSONAL TRAINER

A gym or health club doesn't have to be fancy, but it should have a knowledgeable, cautious, and helpful staff and at least one certified personal trainer on duty at all times. It should have a good selection of aerobic/cardiovascular exercise equipment (treadmills, bikes, stepping machines) as well as resistance training machines and free weights.

It is always better to start out with a monthly or three-month membership to see if the gym or club delivers on its promises to give you a safe, effective, and fun workout.

In choosing a personal trainer, find someone who is willing to give you the names and telephone numbers of satisfied clients. You need someone who can motivate you with his/her enthusiasm and can do a complete health risk assessment before putting you on a fitness program. The trainer should have current cardiopulmonary resuscitation (CPR) certification.

Look for a trainer certified by one of the organizations listed below. Some trainers have multiple certifications which generally give them better knowledge of the variety of exercise concepts.

National Certifying Organizations

- National Academy of Sports Medicine
- American College of Sports Medicine
- American Council on Exercise
- International Association of Fitness Professionals (IDEA)
- The Institute of Aerobics Research
- Aerobics and Fitness Association of America
- National Federation of Professional Trainers
- National Strength and Conditioning Association
- American Aerobic Association/International Sports Medicine Association

WEEK FOUR:
PUTTING IT ALL TOGETHER

Now that you have our resistance exercise down and your body is structurally stronger and more flexible, you can add aerobic/cardiovascular exercise (nonimpact/low impact) three times a week to bring your Total Body Rejuvenation program in total balance for a high-energy, kick-butt, proud to be walking, talking body!

Here is your workout schedule for week four. Remember to go back to the chapter on calculating your target heart rate while performing aerobic/cardiovascular activity to make certain you are exercising correctly and staying in your target heart rate zone.

Note: You now advance to a six-day-per-week routine—three alternate days of resistance exercises and three alternating days of aerobic/cardiovascular activity.

Aerobic/Cardiovascular Exercises:

The information below will help you select aerobic activities best suited for you. They are classified as easy or hard.

Aerobic/cardiovascular exercises that are **easy**:

- Stair Steppers
  A low-impact aerobic exercise that also tones and firms the hips, thighs, and buttocks. If you use a dual action machine, you also tone and firm your upper body. When using a stair stepper, you get resistance up and down.
- Ski Simulators
  An excellent aerobic activity. Cross-country skiing rates highest in lab tests for burning the most calories per minute because you are using your legs, arms, and even your torso. Ski machines can be boring unless using Tony Little's Skier Personal Trainer Video.
- Stationary Bikes
  A nonimpact cardiovascular workout that tones and firms the calves, thighs, hips, and buttocks. If you use dual action, you also tone and firm your upper body. Good for the very overweight because it supports the body weight during exercise.
- Brisk Walking
  An outdoor aerobic activity for those who do not have any other aerobic machines. Fun workout because you get a change in scenery. Remember to walk at a *brisk* pace.
- Swimming
  Great aerobic workout, but because you are buoyant or supported in the water, it is less aerobic than identical movements out of the water. Therefore there is less oxygen consumed and fewer calories are burned. You could exercise harder, but this becomes tiring very fast; fewer calories burned at equivalent work levels equals less fat loss potential.
- Video Step Routines
  Good cardiovascular workout that also tones and firms the hips, legs, and buttocks. Great fat burner because you stay at a low intensity for a longer period of time. Always look for certified instructors and wear proper supportive shoes. Always start at the beginner level and begin with a four- to six-inch step.
- Treadmills
  Great cardiovascular workout because you do it indoors and don't have to worry about weather or muggers. To avoid boredom, work out in front of a TV or with Tony Little's Treadmill Personal Training Video.
- Low Impact Dance
  Less jarring on the joints than traditional high-impact dance and a good cardiovascular workout because you are using large muscle groups to increase your heart rate. Always look for a certified instructor and wear proper supportive shoes.

Aerobic/cardiovascular exercises that are **hard**:

- Climbers
  Climbers (Versa Climbers) work your heart and lungs. The machine is dual action, which works your upper and lower body simultaneously. Tends to be an advanced workout. Fun and challenging.
- Rowers
  A nonimpact cardiovascular activity that works the heart and lungs. It also tones and firms the upper body and torso. Not recommended for anyone with back problems.
- Hiking
  Can be a very dynamic workout, depending upon the type of terrain you choose.
- Jogging
  More impact on the joints than walking, but a good cardiovascular workout. Select good running shoes. Dress properly for the weather. Not recommended for the extremely overweight or those with back problems.

WEEK FOUR:
PUTTING IT ALL TOGETHER

	Date:	NOTE: Don't forget your active warmup and static stretching before your workout.										
SUNDAY OFF	DATE:				DATE:				DATE:			

	MONDAY Upper Body & Lower Body Workout				TUESDAY Abdominal, Back & Aerobic Workout				WEDNESDAY Upper Body & Lower Body Workout			
		WEIGHT	REPS	SET(S)		WEIGHT	REPS	SET(S)		WEIGHT	REPS	SET(S)
	Exercise #5 Modified Squats				Exercise #1 Abdominal Curls				Exercise #5 Modified Squats			
	Exercise #6 Wide Stance Squats				Exercise #2 Reverse Torso Curls				Exercise #6 Wide Stance Squats			
	Exercise #7 Lunges (RT & LT)				Exercise #3 Oblique Curls				Exercise #7 Lunges (RT & LT)			
	Exercise #8 Hip Abduction				Exercise #4 Back Extensions				Exercise #8 Hip Abduction			
	Exercise #9 Hip Adduction				Aerobic/ Cardio-vascular Exercise	Type		Duration	Exercise #9 Hip Adduction			
	Exercise #10 Heel Raises								Exercise #10 Heel Raises			
	Exercise #11 Alternate Toe Raises								Exercise #11 Alternate Toe Raises			
	Exercise #12 Back Rows								Exercise #12 Back Rows			
	Exercise #13 Chest Presses								Exercise #13 Chest Presses			
	Exercise #14 Chest Flyes								Exercise #14 Chest Flyes			
	Exercise #15 Shoulder Presses								Exercise #15 Shoulder Presses			
	Exercise #16 Shoulder Side Raises								Exercise #16 Shoulder Side Raises			
	Exercise #17 Shoulder Front Raises								Exercise #17 Shoulder Front Raises			
	Exercise #18 Triceps Extensions								Exercise #18 Triceps Extensions			
	Exercise #19 Alternate Biceps Curls								Exercise #19 Alternate Biceps Curls			
	Exercise #20 Zottman Curls								Exercise #20 Zottman Curls			

WEEK FOUR:
PUTTING IT ALL TOGETHER

NOTE: Don't forget your active warmup and static stretching before your workout.

DATE:				DATE:				DATE:			
THURSDAY Abdominal, Back & Aerobic Workout				**FRIDAY** Upper Body & Lower Body Workout				**SATURDAY** Abdominal, Back & Aerobic Workout			
	WEIGHT	REPS	SET(S)		WEIGHT	REPS	SET(S)		WEIGHT	REPS	SET(S)
Exercise #1 Abdominal Curls				Exercise #5 Modified Squats				Exercise #1 Abdominal Curls			
Exercise #2 Reverse Torso Curls				Exercise #6 Wide Stance Squats				Exercise #2 Reverse Torso Curls			
Exercise #3 Oblique Curls				Exercise #7 Lunges (RT & LT)				Exercise #3 Oblique Curls			
Exercise #4 Back Extensions				Exercise #8 Hip Abduction				Exercise #4 Back Extensions			
Aerobic/ Cardio- vascular Exercise	Type		Duration	Exercise #9 Hip Adduction				Aerobic/ Cardio- vascular Exercise	Type		Duration
				Exercise #10 Heel Raises							
				Exercise #11 Alternate Toe Raises							
				Exercise #12 Back Rows							
				Exercise #13 Chest Presses							
				Exercise #14 Chest Flyes							
				Exercise #15 Shoulder Presses							
				Exercise #16 Shoulder Side Raises							
				Exercise #17 Shoulder Front Raises							
				Exercise #18 Triceps Extensions							
				Exercise #19 Alternate Biceps Curls							
				Exercise #20 Zottman Curls							

7
Weeks Five through Eight

Your technique is now perfect, so from now on you can concentrate on setting and meeting new goals. During these weeks you'll be increasing the number of repetitions of each exercise and, if you're using weight, increasing the amount. I want you to challenge yourself every time you exercise even if all you can manage is a small variation. Pushing yourself to improve is the only way to keep your body changing from day to day.

I also want you to switch to another type of aerobic/cardiovascular activity at least once a week. If you've been walking, try bicycling (on a stationary or regular outdoor bike) or do a gym or home workout on a stepping or a skiing machine. Variety in this phase of your exercise program is *essential* for the rapid changes in muscle–fat ratio possible on this program. If you don't keep challenging yourself by changing from one type of aerobic/cardiovascular exercise to another, your body will adapt to your workout. You will hit a plateau and won't burn off fat as quickly as you want. Switch from one type of aerobic/cardiovascular exercise to another as often as possible. A change every other workout is ideal. If you can't make a change that often, be sure to switch at least once a week.

Be sure to keep a careful record of your progress on the weekly logs. Note your daily repetitions and sets, the amount of weight you're using for each exercise, and the type and time of your aerobic/cardiovascular workout. Try to increase the duration of your aerobic/cardiovascular workout by five minutes each week. And don't forget to monitor your heart rate. This is particularly important whenever you extend your time. Be sure that you're working in your target zone and that you can hold a conversation while you exercise. If you can't talk comfortably, ease off.

How are you doing with your low-fat eating plan? Continue to keep track of what you eat in the logs on pages 183–192. Did you remember to take your measurements at the end of week four and record them in the log on pages 176 and 177? What a difference!

Your body is becoming a *lean, mean, enjoying life machine.* By now you have lost

180   some fat and felt your body tightening up and your energy level spiraling upward every day. And you're not even halfway through this program yet! Think about how great you'll look and feel next week and a month from now. Success breeds success. You're on the way to where you want to be.

Remember: This is a *progressive* program. Each workout, each additional repetition, each extra pound of weight you use in your resistance training, each minute you add to your aerobic/cardiovascular workout, takes you closer and closer to your goal. Day by day you are getting stronger, leaner, more fit. Keep challenging yourself. That dynamite body is yours if you want it.

Believe in yourself, and everyone else will, too.

DONNA FRUCHON

Scranton, Pennsylvania

Donna's "before" picture was taken on June 10, 1992, her thirty-fifth birthday and the day her daughter graduated from high school. "How I longed to look dynamic," she wrote. "I had always been the youngest mom at school functions." But despite all of her efforts, Donna hadn't been able to lose weight. Worse, her extra weight seemed to worsen a serious problem with asthma.

"The year before I began working out, I tried to shovel the snow off half of my sidewalk. I began to sweat heavily, got weak, and didn't think I could get into the house fast enough. I threw off my coat and scarf and lay flat until I'd recovered enough to take my medication and use my asthma inhaler," Donna recalls.

When she began my workout, Donna was a size 14. She swears that ten "vigorous" days later, she was a size 10. By October 1992 she was an 8. Best of all, her asthma no longer troubles her.

The next winter she shoveled her entire driveway. Afterward, she wrote, "I calmly walked into the house and used my inhaler only once."

"That sure is progress to me. There isn't enough money in the world to make me stop working out. I don't like being sick! I want to be healthy, and I *need* this incredible energy!"

JANET SMITH

Tuckerton, New Jersey

Doesn't Janet Smith look terrific? She's an inspiration to us all.

She was a victim of yo-yo dieting. Now she eats what she wants and looks better than ever.

Here's her story:

"I weighed 288 pounds and was desperately unhappy. I made up my mind to lose the weight and got down to 150 in eighteen months on an 800-calorie-a-day diet. Only sheer determination kept me on it. I did no exercise. Can you picture all that loose skin?

"Six months later I was back to 196 and on my way again."

Then Janet saw me on television and decided to try losing weight and getting in shape my way.

"I could no longer stick to a rigid diet, so I exercised five times a week," she reports. But she got results: she has lost 148 pounds.

Her success has changed her life in many ways. She quit smoking with no weight gain. "Everyone thought my willpower was great (ha!). I was elected to a town position. My self-esteem keeps growing.

"I'm forty-six years old and weigh 140 pounds. I cut all the fat out of my diet except for meat at dinner. Now my size 12 jeans are loose. Can you see I have a collarbone? A hipbone?

"I've never been so happy in my life."

I've said it before and I'll say it again because it's important: You are what you eat. Eat healthy foods and cut the fat!

WEEK FIVE

This stage is essentially a repeat of week four, but you try to increase your weights or number of repetitions for the weight resistance exercises. If you want great results, now's the time to start challenging yourself. Check your previous week's chart and see what you have to do to beat those numbers in order to improve. If one set is not challenging, do a second one. Remember, the key to safe and effective results is *Technique!*

Also select another type of aerobic/cardiovascular exercise or video for this week. Variety is essential for rapid changes in your muscle–fat ratio, and working out is more fun and less boring when you use variety. Variety is truly the spice of life.

Your body and attitude take on a new shape, and you become a *lean, mean, enjoying life machine!*

Another very important point: Follow the nutritional guidelines in this book. You really *"are what you eat"!* Remember what you've learned in Chapter 9.

WEEK SIX,
WEEK SEVEN, AND WEEK EIGHT

During these weeks, you'll follow the same workout routine you've been performing. Refer to week five's weight and repetition numbers so you can set new goals in those areas for even more great changes both physiologically and psychologically, *baby!*

Also, again change your aerobic/cardiovascular selections and increase your time duration by five minutes or longer than last week to increase your fat burning. Be sure to monitor your heart rate. Chart everything and make everything a goal no matter how small.

WEEK FIVE

Date:	NOTE: Don't forget your active warmup and static stretching before your workout.			

<table>
<tr>
<td rowspan="2">SUNDAY
OFF</td>
<td colspan="4">DATE:</td>
<td colspan="4">DATE:</td>
<td colspan="4">DATE:</td>
</tr>
<tr>
<td colspan="4">MONDAY
Upper Body &
Lower Body Workout</td>
<td colspan="4">TUESDAY
Abdominal, Back &
Aerobic Workout</td>
<td colspan="4">WEDNESDAY
Upper Body &
Lower Body Workout</td>
</tr>
<tr>
<td></td>
<td></td><td>WEIGHT</td><td>REPS</td><td>SET(S)</td>
<td></td><td>WEIGHT</td><td>REPS</td><td>SET(S)</td>
<td></td><td>WEIGHT</td><td>REPS</td><td>SET(S)</td>
</tr>
<tr>
<td></td>
<td>Exercise #5
Modified
Squats</td><td></td><td></td><td></td>
<td>Exercise #1
Abdominal
Curls</td><td></td><td></td><td></td>
<td>Exercise #5
Modified
Squats</td><td></td><td></td><td></td>
</tr>
<tr>
<td></td>
<td>Exercise #6
Wide Stance
Squats</td><td></td><td></td><td></td>
<td>Exercise #2
Reverse
Torso Curls</td><td></td><td></td><td></td>
<td>Exercise #6
Wide Stance
Squats</td><td></td><td></td><td></td>
</tr>
<tr>
<td></td>
<td>Exercise #7
Lunges
(RT & LT)</td><td></td><td></td><td></td>
<td>Exercise #3
Oblique
Curls</td><td></td><td></td><td></td>
<td>Exercise #7
Lunges
(RT & LT)</td><td></td><td></td><td></td>
</tr>
<tr>
<td></td>
<td>Exercise #8
Hip
Abduction</td><td></td><td></td><td></td>
<td>Exercise #4
Back
Extensions</td><td></td><td></td><td></td>
<td>Exercise #8
Hip
Abduction</td><td></td><td></td><td></td>
</tr>
<tr>
<td></td>
<td>Exercise #9
Hip
Adduction</td><td></td><td></td><td></td>
<td>Aerobic/
Cardio-
vascular
Exercise</td><td colspan="2">Type</td><td>Duration</td>
<td>Exercise #9
Hip
Adduction</td><td></td><td></td><td></td>
</tr>
<tr>
<td></td>
<td>Exercise #10
Heel
Raises</td><td></td><td></td><td></td>
<td></td><td></td><td></td><td></td>
<td>Exercise #10
Heel
Raises</td><td></td><td></td><td></td>
</tr>
<tr>
<td></td>
<td>Exercise #11
Alternate
Toe Raises</td><td></td><td></td><td></td>
<td></td><td></td><td></td><td></td>
<td>Exercise #11
Alternate
Toe Raises</td><td></td><td></td><td></td>
</tr>
<tr>
<td></td>
<td>Exercise #12
Back Rows</td><td></td><td></td><td></td>
<td></td><td></td><td></td><td></td>
<td>Exercise #12
Back Rows</td><td></td><td></td><td></td>
</tr>
<tr>
<td></td>
<td>Exercise #13
Chest
Presses</td><td></td><td></td><td></td>
<td></td><td></td><td></td><td></td>
<td>Exercise #13
Chest
Presses</td><td></td><td></td><td></td>
</tr>
<tr>
<td></td>
<td>Exercise #14
Chest
Flyes</td><td></td><td></td><td></td>
<td></td><td></td><td></td><td></td>
<td>Exercise #14
Chest
Flyes</td><td></td><td></td><td></td>
</tr>
<tr>
<td></td>
<td>Exercise #15
Shoulder
Presses</td><td></td><td></td><td></td>
<td></td><td></td><td></td><td></td>
<td>Exercise #15
Shoulder
Presses</td><td></td><td></td><td></td>
</tr>
<tr>
<td></td>
<td>Exercise #16
Shoulder
Side Raises</td><td></td><td></td><td></td>
<td></td><td></td><td></td><td></td>
<td>Exercise #16
Shoulder
Side Raises</td><td></td><td></td><td></td>
</tr>
<tr>
<td></td>
<td>Exercise #17
Shoulder
Front Raises</td><td></td><td></td><td></td>
<td></td><td></td><td></td><td></td>
<td>Exercise #17
Shoulder
Front Raises</td><td></td><td></td><td></td>
</tr>
<tr>
<td></td>
<td>Exercise #18
Triceps
Extensions</td><td></td><td></td><td></td>
<td></td><td></td><td></td><td></td>
<td>Exercise #18
Triceps
Extensions</td><td></td><td></td><td></td>
</tr>
<tr>
<td></td>
<td>Exercise #19
Alternate
Biceps Curls</td><td></td><td></td><td></td>
<td></td><td></td><td></td><td></td>
<td>Exercise #19
Alternate
Biceps Curls</td><td></td><td></td><td></td>
</tr>
<tr>
<td></td>
<td>Exercise #20
Zottman
Curls</td><td></td><td></td><td></td>
<td></td><td></td><td></td><td></td>
<td>Exercise #20
Zottman
Curls</td><td></td><td></td><td></td>
</tr>
</table>

WEEK FIVE

NOTE: Don't forget your active warmup and static stretching before your workout.

DATE:				DATE:				DATE:			
THURSDAY Abdominal, Back & Aerobic Workout				**FRIDAY** Upper Body & Lower Body Workout				**SATURDAY** Abdominal, Back & Aerobic Workout			
	WEIGHT	REPS	SET(S)		WEIGHT	REPS	SET(S)		WEIGHT	REPS	SET(S)
Exercise #1 Abdominal Curls				Exercise #5 Modified Squats				Exercise #1 Abdominal Curls			
Exercise #2 Reverse Torso Curls				Exercise #6 Wide Stance Squats				Exercise #2 Reverse Torso Curls			
Exercise #3 Oblique Curls				Exercise #7 Lunges (RT & LT)				Exercise #3 Oblique Curls			
Exercise #4 Back Extensions				Exercise #8 Hip Abduction				Exercise #4 Back Extensions			
Aerobic/ Cardio- vascular Exercise	Type		Duration	Exercise #9 Hip Adduction				Aerobic/ Cardio- vascular Exercise	Type		Duration
				Exercise #10 Heel Raises							
				Exercise #11 Alternate Toe Raises							
				Exercise #12 Back Rows							
				Exercise #13 Chest Presses							
				Exercise #14 Chest Flyes							
				Exercise #15 Shoulder Presses							
				Exercise #16 Shoulder Side Raises							
				Exercise #17 Shoulder Front Raises							
				Exercise #18 Triceps Extensions							
				Exercise #19 Alternate Biceps Curls							
				Exercise #20 Zottman Curls							

WEEK SIX

| Date: | NOTE: Don't forget your active warmup and static stretching before your workout. | | | | | | | | | | | |

DATE:				DATE:				DATE:			
MONDAY Upper Body & Lower Body Workout				**TUESDAY** Abdominal, Back & Aerobic Workout				**WEDNESDAY** Upper Body & Lower Body Workout			
	WEIGHT	REPS	SET(S)		WEIGHT	REPS	SET(S)		WEIGHT	REPS	SET(S)
Exercise #5 Modified Squats				Exercise #1 Abdominal Curls				Exercise #5 Modified Squats			
Exercise #6 Wide Stance Squats				Exercise #2 Reverse Torso Curls				Exercise #6 Wide Stance Squats			
Exercise #7 Lunges (RT & LT)				Exercise #3 Oblique Curls				Exercise #7 Lunges (RT & LT)			
Exercise #8 Hip Abduction				Exercise #4 Back Extensions				Exercise #8 Hip Abduction			
Exercise #9 Hip Adduction				Aerobic/ Cardio-vascular Exercise	Type		Duration	Exercise #9 Hip Adduction			
Exercise #10 Heel Raises								Exercise #10 Heel Raises			
Exercise #11 Alternate Toe Raises								Exercise #11 Alternate Toe Raises			
Exercise #12 Back Rows								Exercise #12 Back Rows			
Exercise #13 Chest Presses								Exercise #13 Chest Presses			
Exercise #14 Chest Flyes								Exercise #14 Chest Flyes			
Exercise #15 Shoulder Presses								Exercise #15 Shoulder Presses			
Exercise #16 Shoulder Side Raises								Exercise #16 Shoulder Side Raises			
Exercise #17 Shoulder Front Raises								Exercise #17 Shoulder Front Raises			
Exercise #18 Triceps Extensions								Exercise #18 Triceps Extensions			
Exercise #19 Alternate Biceps Curls								Exercise #19 Alternate Biceps Curls			
Exercise #20 Zottman Curls								Exercise #20 Zottman Curls			

WEEK SIX

NOTE: Don't forget your active warmup and static stretching before your workout.

DATE:				DATE:				DATE:			
THURSDAY Abdominal, Back & Aerobic Workout				**FRIDAY** Upper Body & Lower Body Workout				**SATURDAY** Abdominal, Back & Aerobic Workout			
	WEIGHT	REPS	SET(S)		WEIGHT	REPS	SET(S)		WEIGHT	REPS	SET(S)
Exercise #1 Abdominal Curls				Exercise #5 Modified Squats				Exercise #1 Abdominal Curls			
Exercise #2 Reverse Torso Curls				Exercise #6 Wide Stance Squats				Exercise #2 Reverse Torso Curls			
Exercise #3 Oblique Curls				Exercise #7 Lunges (RT & LT)				Exercise #3 Oblique Curls			
Exercise #4 Back Extensions				Exercise #8 Hip Abduction				Exercise #4 Back Extensions			
Aerobic/ Cardio- vascular Exercise	Type		Duration	Exercise #9 Hip Adduction				Aerobic/ Cardio- vascular Exercise	Type		Duration
				Exercise #10 Heel Raises							
				Exercise #11 Alternate Toe Raises							
				Exercise #12 Back Rows							
				Exercise #13 Chest Presses							
				Exercise #14 Chest Flyes							
				Exercise #15 Shoulder Presses							
				Exercise #16 Shoulder Side Raises							
				Exercise #17 Shoulder Front Raises							
				Exercise #18 Triceps Extensions							
				Exercise #19 Alternate Biceps Curls							
				Exercise #20 Zottman Curls							

WEEK SEVEN

Date:	NOTE: Don't forget your active warmup and static stretching before your workout.

SUNDAY OFF	DATE:				DATE:				DATE:			
	MONDAY Upper Body & Lower Body Workout				**TUESDAY** Abdominal, Back & Aerobic Workout				**WEDNESDAY** Upper Body & Lower Body Workout			
		WEIGHT	REPS	SET(S)		WEIGHT	REPS	SET(S)		WEIGHT	REPS	SET(S)
	Exercise #5 Modified Squats				Exercise #1 Abdominal Curls				Exercise #5 Modified Squats			
	Exercise #6 Wide Stance Squats				Exercise #2 Reverse Torso Curls				Exercise #6 Wide Stance Squats			
	Exercise #7 Lunges (RT & LT)				Exercise #3 Oblique Curls				Exercise #7 Lunges (RT & LT)			
	Exercise #8 Hip Abduction				Exercise #4 Back Extensions				Exercise #8 Hip Abduction			
	Exercise #9 Hip Adduction				Aerobic/ Cardio-vascular Exercise	Type	Duration		Exercise #9 Hip Adduction			
	Exercise #10 Heel Raises								Exercise #10 Heel Raises			
	Exercise #11 Alternate Toe Raises								Exercise #11 Alternate Toe Raises			
	Exercise #12 Back Rows								Exercise #12 Back Rows			
	Exercise #13 Chest Presses								Exercise #13 Chest Presses			
	Exercise #14 Chest Flyes								Exercise #14 Chest Flyes			
	Exercise #15 Shoulder Presses								Exercise #15 Shoulder Presses			
	Exercise #16 Shoulder Side Raises								Exercise #16 Shoulder Side Raises			
	Exercise #17 Shoulder Front Raises								Exercise #17 Shoulder Front Raises			
	Exercise #18 Triceps Extensions								Exercise #18 Triceps Extensions			
	Exercise #19 Alternate Biceps Curls								Exercise #19 Alternate Biceps Curls			
	Exercise #20 Zottman Curls								Exercise #20 Zottman Curls			

WEEK SEVEN

NOTE: Don't forget your active warmup and static stretching before your workout.

DATE:				DATE:				DATE:			
THURSDAY Abdominal, Back & Aerobic Workout				**FRIDAY** Upper Body & Lower Body Workout				**SATURDAY** Abdominal, Back & Aerobic Workout			
	WEIGHT	REPS	SET(S)		WEIGHT	REPS	SET(S)		WEIGHT	REPS	SET(S)
Exercise #1 Abdominal Curls				Exercise #5 Modified Squats				Exercise #1 Abdominal Curls			
Exercise #2 Reverse Torso Curls				Exercise #6 Wide Stance Squats				Exercise #2 Reverse Torso Curls			
Exercise #3 Oblique Curls				Exercise #7 Lunges (RT & LT)				Exercise #3 Oblique Curls			
Exercise #4 Back Extensions				Exercise #8 Hip Abduction				Exercise #4 Back Extensions			
Aerobic/ Cardio- vascular Exercise	Type	Duration		Exercise #9 Hip Adduction				Aerobic/ Cardio- vascular Exercise	Type	Duration	
				Exercise #10 Heel Raises							
				Exercise #11 Alternate Toe Raises							
				Exercise #12 Back Rows							
				Exercise #13 Chest Presses							
				Exercise #14 Chest Flyes							
				Exercise #15 Shoulder Presses							
				Exercise #16 Shoulder Side Raises							
				Exercise #17 Shoulder Front Raises							
				Exercise #18 Triceps Extensions							
				Exercise #19 Alternate Biceps Curls							
				Exercise #20 Zottman Curls							

WEEK EIGHT

Date:	NOTE: Don't forget your active warmup and static stretching before your workout.

SUNDAY OFF

	DATE:				DATE:				DATE:			
	MONDAY Upper Body & Lower Body Workout				**TUESDAY** Abdominal, Back & Aerobic Workout				**WEDNESDAY** Upper Body & Lower Body Workout			
		WEIGHT	REPS	SET(S)		WEIGHT	REPS	SET(S)		WEIGHT	REPS	SET(S)
	Exercise #5 Modified Squats				Exercise #1 Abdominal Curls				Exercise #5 Modified Squats			
	Exercise #6 Wide Stance Squats				Exercise #2 Reverse Torso Curls				Exercise #6 Wide Stance Squats			
	Exercise #7 Lunges (RT & LT)				Exercise #3 Oblique Curls				Exercise #7 Lunges (RT & LT)			
	Exercise #8 Hip Abduction				Exercise #4 Back Extensions				Exercise #8 Hip Abduction			
	Exercise #9 Hip Adduction				Aerobic/ Cardio- vascular Exercise	Type		Duration	Exercise #9 Hip Adduction			
	Exercise #10 Heel Raises								Exercise #10 Heel Raises			
	Exercise #11 Alternate Toe Raises								Exercise #11 Alternate Toe Raises			
	Exercise #12 Back Rows								Exercise #12 Back Rows			
	Exercise #13 Chest Presses								Exercise #13 Chest Presses			
	Exercise #14 Chest Flyes								Exercise #14 Chest Flyes			
	Exercise #15 Shoulder Presses								Exercise #15 Shoulder Presses			
	Exercise #16 Shoulder Side Raises								Exercise #16 Shoulder Side Raises			
	Exercise #17 Shoulder Front Raises								Exercise #17 Shoulder Front Raises			
	Exercise #18 Triceps Extensions								Exercise #18 Triceps Extensions			
	Exercise #19 Alternate Biceps Curls								Exercise #19 Alternate Biceps Curls			
	Exercise #20 Zottman Curls								Exercise #20 Zottman Curls			

WEEK EIGHT

NOTE: Don't forget your active warmup and static stretching before your workout.

DATE:				DATE:				DATE:			
THURSDAY Abdominal, Back & Aerobic Workout				**FRIDAY** Upper Body & Lower Body Workout				**SATURDAY** Abdominal, Back & Aerobic Workout			
	WEIGHT	REPS	SET(S)		WEIGHT	REPS	SET(S)		WEIGHT	REPS	SET(S)
Exercise #1 Abdominal Curls				Exercise #5 Modified Squats				Exercise #1 Abdominal Curls			
Exercise #2 Reverse Torso Curls				Exercise #6 Wide Stance Squats				Exercise #2 Reverse Torso Curls			
Exercise #3 Oblique Curls				Exercise #7 Lunges (RT & LT)				Exercise #3 Oblique Curls			
Exercise #4 Back Extensions				Exercise #8 Hip Abduction				Exercise #4 Back Extensions			
Aerobic/ Cardio- vascular Exercise	Type	Duration		Exercise #9 Hip Adduction				Aerobic/ Cardio- vascular Exercise	Type	Duration	
				Exercise #10 Heel Raises							
				Exercise #11 Alternate Toe Raises							
				Exercise #12 Back Rows							
				Exercise #13 Chest Presses							
				Exercise #14 Chest Flyes							
				Exercise #15 Shoulder Presses							
				Exercise #16 Shoulder Side Raises							
				Exercise #17 Shoulder Front Raises							
				Exercise #18 Triceps Extensions							
				Exercise #19 Alternate Biceps Curls							
				Exercise #20 Zottman Curls							

8
Weeks Nine through Sixteen

Beginning with week nine, I'm going to make some important changes in your training schedule. You'll be adding an extra session of aerobic/cardiovascular activity, varying your strength training routine, and working out with heavier weights.

You also will take a break every fourth day instead of on Sunday.

Your new schedule is called a **split routine.** Here's my plan:

Monday: Abdominals, lower body exercises, and your aerobic/cardiovascular workout.

Tuesday: Upper body exercises plus aerobic/cardiovascular workouts.

Wednesday: Abdominals and lower body exercises.

Thursday: Off.

Friday: Abdominal, upper body, and aerobic/cardiovascular.

Saturday: Lower body abdominals and aerobic/cardiovascular.

Sunday: Upper body.

Monday: Off.

Tuesday: Lower body abdominals and aerobic/cardiovascular.

And so on.

MARTIN CHIANI

Levittown, New York

Before he found my workout program, Martin had been a victim of the yo-yo syndrome. "I would lose the weight, but it took me six months to do it. Not only did I look sickly, but the weight came back twice as fast." He tried exercising at health spas but never got on the right track: "No one showed me how to use the machines properly, and all the exercises I had learned in school were all wrong."

He began my program in August of 1993. By October he'd lost almost thirty pounds and had started to firm up and develop muscles. "I look and feel better at forty-one than I did at twenty-nine," he writes.

Martin is a nursing student with lots of reading to do after classes, so he didn't have much time to exercise. He also has a back and knee problem, so my low-impact program was ideal. He hasn't had a single injury.

Martin's only complaint is that the program works too well: "I had to keep buying new clothes because my old ones wouldn't fit. They were all too big! Now my metabolism is up and I can eat whatever I want whenever I want. This program is the only one I've found that works!"

You can't argue with results. Martin got them, and he got them fast!

> **TIP:** You don't have to stick to the schedule above for your abdominal/back exercises. Just be sure to do them three times a week.

The most obvious change from your earlier workouts is that you'll be doing your aerobic/cardiovascular workout more often: four days a week instead of three. By now you are ready to increase your *minimum* aerobic/cardiovascular workout to twenty-five minutes per session. Your *maximum* aerobic/cardiovascular time should be sixty minutes per workout in addition to your warm-up, stretching, and cooldown. Whether you're doing the minimum or maximum aerobic/cardiovascular workout, you must continue to monitor your heart rate to make sure you are in your target zone.

> **TIP:** You don't have to do your aerobic/cardiovascular and resistance training workouts at the same time. You can do one workout in the morning and the other later in the day. If you do them at the same time, you can use your aerobic/cardiovascular workout as the warm-up for your resistance training exercises.

I also want you to increase the number of *sets* per exercise from one to two for each body part. To keep from getting bored, vary the order of exercises you do during your upper and lower body workouts.

Another big change: You'll be using weights differently from now on. Now that you're doing two sets per exercise. I want you to use a slightly heavier weight for your second set. The first set will warm up your muscles and draw upon a certain amount of muscle cells. By adding weight during the second set, you call upon even more muscle cells. With this system you begin to maximize and build muscle strength and size.

Even though you'll be increasing the weight from set to set (called **pyramiding**), *never* sacrifice technique. If you can't do the exercise properly with additional weight, you're using too much. Gauge the correct amount of weight for your individual needs by the number of repetitions you can perform with perfect technique. You're working at the right weight when the last few repetitions of the second set are challenging but still possible with perfect technique. If your goal is to lose weight and you can only do five repetitions or less with the heavier weight, *immediately* go back to the weight you used for your first set and finish out the second set.

Now that you've reached this most challenging level of your Total Body Rejuvenation program, you're going to see tremendous changes in your body. You'll be burning more calories through exercise than you did earlier in this program because you are doing your aerobic/cardiovascular workout more often and because your minimum time is longer. Don't forget to vary your aerobic/cardiovascular activity. Just because you're working longer and harder doesn't mean your body won't adapt to any given activity.

196 You must continue to challenge yourself by switching from one type of exercise to another. If you don't, you can hit a frustrating plateau and will see no changes in your body for weeks at a time.

You'll also be building lean muscle tissue at a faster rate as a result of your more intense resistance training workout, and now you can fully appreciate what lean muscle means: higher metabolism, more fat burning, and higher energy levels.

This final phase of your training program gives you a workout that will last you a lifetime and enable you to *maintain* the lean, muscular, beautiful body you always wanted. By this point in the program you'll see major changes in your body and attitude. You can sense that your goal is within reach. You'll be stronger, more fit, leaner. You will have lost inches, and your body will be firmer, tighter, and more youthful looking than ever.

The challenges in the weeks ahead will speed you toward the body of your dreams. You are ready for them. You have mastered technique. Having come this far, you have new energy and a more positive attitude. You've seen the results of a progressive program. Step by step, day by day, over the past eight weeks you've shown what you can do. You can be very proud of your achievements. But you'll be prouder still by the time you reach week sixteen.

I knew you could do it. You're conceiving! You're believing! You're achieving!

MICHAEL AND KIM RYAN

Hackettstown, New Jersey

Michael and Kim Ryan are two of my favorite people. I've gotten to know them well since they first wrote to tell me about their success with my workout program.

Their son, Jake, was Kim's inspiration for getting in shape. "I didn't want him growing up with a fat mommy," she wrote.

Kim weighed more than 220 pounds when she decided to shape up. Michael weighed 263. After a year of my workout program, Kim lost eighty-six pounds and is now a svelte size 8. "I didn't add up the inches I lost, but it's probably a whole other person," says Kim. Michael had dropped forty-five pounds. He hasn't been in such good shape since high school.

They look great. When Jake sees that "before" photo, he's going to be very proud of his mom and dad.

WEEKS NINE THROUGH TWELVE: WORKOUT CHARTS

During this phase of your training, alter your schedule so that over a three-day consecutive period you are alternating between upper body and aerobics one day and lower body and aerobics the next, with the fourth day off. This is called a split routine.

During this phase you also add more sets per exercise so that you're performing two sets per body part, utilizing several different exercises. Never use the same order of exercises for a body part all the time. Variety of exercise sequence within a body part is the key here.

Pyramiding the weight you use is also a part of this phase. Try to increase the weight slightly from set to set in order to speed the rate at which you stimulate/fatigue the specific muscle. Never sacrifice technique for heavier weight. Both men and women can pyramid weight.

Increase your aerobic activity time, too. Your minimum is now twenty-five minutes. (Keep in mind that you still must monitor your target heart rate.)

Note: You don't have to do your aerobics and resistance exercise workout at the same time. You can do the aerobics in the morning and the resistance exercises in the evening or use your aerobic workout as your active warm-up and then go right into your resistance exercises.

CONCEIVE!! BELIEVE!! ACHIEVE!!
TRAIN HARD, THINK COOL, LOOK HOT!

WEEK NINE

NOTE: Don't forget your active warmup and static stretching before your workout.

DATE:	DATE:				DATE:			
SUNDAY OFF	**MONDAY** Abdominal, Back, Lower Body & Aerobic Workout				**TUESDAY** Upper Body & Aerobic Workout			
		WEIGHT	REPS	SET(S)		WEIGHT	REPS	SET(S)
	Exercise #1 Abdominal Curls				Exercise #12 Back Rows			
	Exercise #2 Reverse Torso Curls				Exercise #13 Chest Presses			
	Exercise #3 Oblique Curls				Exercise #14 Chest Flyes			
	Exercise #4 Back Extensions				Exercise #15 Shoulder Press			
	Exercise #5 Modified Squats				Exercise #16 Shoulder Side Raises			
	Exercise #6 Wide Stance Squats				Exercise #17 Shoulder Front Raises			
	Exercise #7 Lunges (RT & LT)				Exercise #18 Triceps Extensions			
	Exercise #8 Hip Abduction				Exercise #19 Alternate Biceps Curls			
	Exercise #9 Hip Adduction				Exercise #20 Zottman Curls			
	Exercise #10 Heel Raises				Aerobic/ Cardio-vascular Exercise	Type	Duration	
	Exercise #11 Alternate Toe Raises							
	Aerobic/ Cardio-vascular Exercise	Type	Duration					

WEEK NINE

NOTE: Don't forget your active warmup and static stretching before your workout.

DATE:				DATE:	DATE:			
WEDNESDAY Abdominal, Back & Lower Body Workout				THURSDAY OFF	**FRIDAY** Abdominal, Back, Lower Body & Aerobic Workout			
	WEIGHT	REPS	SET(S)			WEIGHT	REPS	SET(S)
Exercise #1 Abdominal Curls					Exercise #1 Abdominal Curls			
Exercise #2 Reverse Torso Curls					Exercise #2 Reverse Torso Curls			
Exercise #3 Oblique Curls					Exercise #3 Oblique Curls			
Exercise #4 Back Extensions					Exercise #4 Back Extensions			
Exercise #5 Modified Squats					Exercise #5 Modified Squats			
Exercise #6 Wide Stance Squats					Exercise #6 Wide Stance Squats			
Exercise #7 Lunges (RT & LT)					Exercise #7 Lunges (RT & LT)			
Exercise #8 Hip Abduction					Exercise #8 Hip Abduction			
Exercise #9 Hip Adduction					Exercise #9 Hip Adduction			
Exercise #10 Heel Raises					Exercise #10 Heel Raises			
Exercise #11 Alternate Toe Raises					Exercise #11 Alternate Toe Raises			
					Aerobic/ Cardio- vascular Exercise	Type		Duration

WEEK NINE

NOTE: Don't forget your active warmup and static stretching before your workout

DATE:				DATE:				DATE:
SATURDAY Upper Body & Aerobic Workout				**SUNDAY** Abdominal, Back & Lower Body Workout				MONDAY OFF
	WEIGHT	REPS	SET(S)		WEIGHT	REPS	SET(S)	
Exercise #12 Back Rows				Exercise #1 Abdominal Curls				
Exercise #13 Chest Presses				Exercise #2 Reverse Torso Curls				
Exercise #14 Chest Flyes				Exercise #3 Oblique Curls				
Exercise #15 Shoulder Presses				Exercise #4 Back Extensions				
Exercise #16 Shoulder Side Raises				Exercise #5 Modified Squats				
Exercise #17 Shoulder Front Raises				Exercise #6 Wide Stance Squats				
Exercise #18 Triceps Extensions				Exercise #7 Lunges (RT & LT)				
Exercise #19 Alternate Biceps Curls				Exercise #8 Hip Abduction				
Exercise #20 Zottman Curls				Exercise #9 Hip Adduction				
Aerobic/ Cardio- vascular Exercise	Type		Duration	Exercise #10 Heel Raises				
				Exercise #11 Alternate Toe Raises				

WEEK TEN

NOTE: Don't forget your active warmup and static stretching before your workout.

DATE:				DATE:			
TUESDAY Abdominal, Back, Lower Body & Aerobic Workout				**WEDNESDAY** Upper Body & Aerobic Workout			
	WEIGHT	REPS	SET(S)		WEIGHT	REPS	SET(S)
Exercise #1 Abdominal Curls				Exercise #12 Back Rows			
Exercise #2 Reverse Torso Curls				Exercise #13 Chest Presses			
Exercise #3 Oblique Curls				Exercise #14 Chest Flyes			
Exercise #4 Back Extensions				Exercise #15 Shoulder Presses			
Exercise #5 Modified Squats				Exercise #16 Shoulder Side Raises			
Exercise #6 Wide Stance Squats				Exercise #17 Shoulder Front Raises			
Exercise #7 Lunges (RT & LT)				Exercise #18 Triceps Extensions			
Exercise #8 Hip Abduction				Exercise #19 Alternate Biceps Curls			
Exercise #9 Hip Adduction				Exercise #20 Zottman Curls			
Exercise #10 Heel Raises				Aerobic/ Cardio- vascular Exercise	Type	Duration	
Exercise #11 Alternate Toe Raises							
Aerobic/ Cardio- vascular Exercise	Type	Duration					

WEEK TEN

NOTE: Don't forget your active warmup and static stretching before your workout.

DATE:				DATE:	DATE:			
THURSDAY Abdominal, Back & Lower Body Workout				FRIDAY OFF	**SATURDAY** Abdominal, Back, Lower Body & Aerobic Workout			
	WEIGHT	REPS	SET(S)			WEIGHT	REPS	SET(S)
Exercise #1 Abdominal Curls					Exercise #1 Abdominal Curls			
Exercise #2 Reverse Torso Curls					Exercise #2 Reverse Torso Curls			
Exercise #3 Oblique Curls					Exercise #3 Oblique Curls			
Exercise #4 Back Extensions					Exercise #4 Back Extensions			
Exercise #5 Modified Squats					Exercise #5 Modified Squats			
Exercise #6 Wide Stance Squats					Exercise #6 Wide Stance Squats			
Exercise #7 Lungs (RT & LT)					Exercise #7 Lunges (RT & LT)			
Exercise #8 Hip Abduction					Exercise #8 Hip Abduction			
Exercise #9 Hip Adduction					Exercise #9 Hip Adduction			
Exercise #10 Heel Raises					Exercise #10 Heel Raises			
Exercise #11 Alternate Toe Raises					Exercise #11 Alternate Toe Raises			
					Aerobic/ Cardio- vascular Exercise	Type	Duration	

WEEK ELEVEN

NOTE: Don't forget your active warmup and static stretching before your workout.

DATE:				DATE:				DATE:
SUNDAY Upper Body & Aerobic Workout				**MONDAY** Abdominal, Back & Lower Body Workout				TUESDAY OFF
	WEIGHT	REPS	SET(S)		WEIGHT	REPS	SET(S)	
Exercise #12 Back Rows				Exercise #1 Abdominal Curls				
Exercise #13 Chest Presses				Exercise #2 Reverse Torso Curls				
Exercise #14 Chest Flyes				Exercise #3 Oblique Curls				
Exercise #15 Shoulder Presses				Exercise #4 Back Extensions				
Exercise #16 Shoulder Side Raises				Exercise #5 Modified Squats				
Exercise #17 Shoulder Front Raises				Exercise #6 Wide Stance Squats				
Exercise #18 Triceps Extensions				Exercise #7 Lunges (RT & LT)				
Exercise #19 Alternate Biceps Curls				Exercise #8 Hip Abduction				
Exercise #20 Zottman Curls				Exercise #9 Hip Adduction				
Aerobic/ Cardio- vascular Exercise	Type		Duration	Exercise #10 Heel Raises				
				Exercise #11 Alternate Toe Raises				

WEEK ELEVEN

NOTE: Don't forget your active warmup and static stretching before your workout.

DATE:				DATE:			
WEDNESDAY Abdominal, Back, Lower Body & Aerobic Workout				**THURSDAY** Upper Body & Aerobic Workout			
	WEIGHT	REPS	SET(S)		WEIGHT	REPS	SET(S)
Exercise #1 Abdominal Curls				Exercise #12 Back Rows			
Exercise #2 Reverse Torso Curls				Exercise #13 Chest Presses			
Exercise #3 Oblique Curls				Exercise #14 Chest Flyes			
Exercise #4 Back Extensions				Exercise #15 Shoulder Presses			
Exercise #5 Modified Squats				Exercise #16 Shoulder Side Raises			
Exercise #6 Wide Stance Squats				Exercise #17 Shoulder Front Raises			
Exercise #7 Lunges (RT & LT)				Exercise #18 Triceps Extensions			
Exercise #8 Hip Abduction				Exercise #19 Alternate Biceps Curls			
Exercise #9 Hip Adduction				Exercise #20 Zottman Curls			
Exercise #10 Heel Raises				Aerobic/ Cardio- vascular Exercise	Type	Duration	
Exercise #11 Alternate Toe Raises							
Aerobic/ Cardio- vascular Exercise	Type	Duration					

WEEK ELEVEN

NOTE: Don't forget your active warmup and static stretching before your workout.

DATE:				DATE:	DATE:			
FRIDAY Abdominal, Back & Lower Body Workout				SATURDAY OFF	**SUNDAY** Abdominal, Back, Lower Body & Aerobic Workout			
	WEIGHT	REPS	SET(S)			WEIGHT	REPS	SET(S)
Exercise #1 Abdominal Curls					Exercise #1 Abdominal Curls			
Exercise #2 Reverse Torso Curls					Exercise #2 Reverse Torso Curls			
Exercise #3 Oblique Curls					Exercise #3 Oblique Curls			
Exercise #4 Back Extensions					Exercise #4 Back Extensions			
Exercise #5 Modified Squats					Exercise #5 Modified Squats			
Exercise #6 Wide Stance Squats					Exercise #6 Wide Stance Squats			
Exercise #7 Lunges (RT & LT)					Exercise #7 Lunges (RT & LT)			
Exercise #8 Hip Abduction					Exercise #8 Hip Abduction			
Exercise #9 Hip Adduction					Exercise #9 Hip Adduction			
Exercise #10 Heel Raises					Exercise #10 Heel Raises			
Exercise #11 Alternate Toe Raises					Exercise #11 Alternate Toe Raises			
					Aerobic/ Cardio- vascular Exercise	Type	Duration	

WEEK TWELVE

NOTE: Don't forget your active warmup and static stretching before your workout.

DATE:				DATE:				DATE:
MONDAY Upper Body & Aerobic Workout				**TUESDAY** Abdominal, Back & Lower Body Workout				WEDNESDAY OFF
	WEIGHT	REPS	SET(S)		WEIGHT	REPS	SET(S)	
Exercise #12 Back Rows				Exercise #1 Abdominal Curls				
Exercise #13 Chest Presses				Exercise #2 Reverse Torso Curls				
Exercise #14 Chest Flyes				Exercise #3 Oblique Curls				
Exercise #15 Shoulder Presses				Exercise #4 Back Extensions				
Exercise #16 Shoulder Side Raises				Exercise #5 Modified Squats				
Exercise #17 Shoulder Front Raises				Exercise #6 Wide Stance Squats				
Exercise #18 Triceps Extensions				Exercise #7 Lunges (RT & LT)				
Exercise #19 Alternate Biceps Curls				Exercise #8 Hip Abduction				
Exercise #20 Zottman Curls				Exercise #9 Hip Adduction				
Aerobic/ Cardio- vascular Exercise	Type		Duration	Exercise #10 Heel Raises				
				Exercise #11 Alternate Toe Raises				

WEEK TWELVE

NOTE: Don't forget your active warmup and static stretching before your workout.

DATE:				DATE:			
THURSDAY Abdominal, Back, Lower Body & Aerobic Workout				**FRIDAY** Upper Body & Aerobic Workout			
	WEIGHT	REPS	SET(S)		WEIGHT	REPS	SET(S)
Exercise #1 Abdominal Curls				Exercise #12 Back Rows			
Exercise #2 Reverse Torso Curls				Exercise #13 Chest Presses			
Exercise #3 Oblique Curls				Exercise #14 Chest Flyes			
Exercise #4 Back Extensions				Exercise #15 Shoulder Presses			
Exercise #5 Modified Squats				Exercise #16 Shoulder Side Raises			
Exercise #6 Wide Stance Squats				Exercise #17 Shoulder Front Raises			
Exercise #7 Lunges (RT & LT)				Exercise #18 Triceps Extensions			
Exercise #8 Hip Abduction				Exercise #19 Alternate Biceps Curls			
Exercise #9 Hip Adduction				Exercise #20 Zottman Curls			
Exercise #10 Heel Raises				Aerobic/ Cardio- vascular Exercise	Type		Duration
Exercise #11 Alternate Toe Raises							
Aerobic/ Cardio- vascular Exercise	Type		Duration				

WEEK TWELVE

NOTE: Don't forget your active warmup and static stretching before your workout.

DATE:				DATE:	DATE:			
SATURDAY Abdominal, Back & Lower Body Workout				SUNDAY OFF	**MONDAY** Abdominal, Back, Lower Body & Aerobic Workout			
	WEIGHT	REPS	SET(S)			WEIGHT	REPS	SET(S)
Exercise #1 Abdominal Curls					Exercise #1 Abdominal Curls			
Exercise #2 Reverse Torso Curls					Exercise #2 Reverse Torso Curls			
Exercise #3 Oblique Curls					Exercise #3 Oblique Curls			
Exercise #4 Back Extensions					Exercise #4 Back Extensions			
Exercise #5 Modified Squats					Exercise #5 Modified Squats			
Exercise #6 Wide Stance Squats					Exercise #6 Wide Stance Squats			
Exercise #7 Lungs (RT & LT)					Exercise #7 Lunges (RT & LT)			
Exercise #8 Hip Abduction					Exercise #8 Hip Abduction			
Exercise #9 Hip Adduction					Exercise #9 Hip Adduction			
Exercise #10 Heel Raises					Exercise #10 Heel Raises			
Exercise #11 Alternate Toe Raises					Exercise #11 Alternate Toe Raises			
					Aerobic/ Cardio-vascular Exercise	Type	Duration	

WEEK THIRTEEN

NOTE: Don't forget your active warmup and static stretching before your workout.

DATE:				DATE:				DATE:
TUESDAY Upper Body & Aerobic Workout				**WEDNESDAY** Abdominal, Back & Lower Body Workout				THURSDAY OFF
	WEIGHT	REPS	SET(S)		WEIGHT	REPS	SET(S)	
Exercise #12 Back Rows				Exercise #1 Abdominal Curls				
Exercise #13 Chest Presses				Exercise #2 Reverse Torso Curls				
Exercise #14 Chest Flyes				Exercise #3 Oblique Curls				
Exercise #15 Shoulder Presses				Exercise #4 Back Extensions				
Exercise #16 Shoulder Side Raises				Exercise #5 Modified Squats				
Exercise #17 Shoulder Front Raises				Exercise #6 Wide Stance Squats				
Exercise #18 Triceps Extensions				Exercise #7 Lunges (RT & LT)				
Exercise #19 Alternate Biceps Curls				Exercise #8 Hip Abduction				
Exercise #20 Zottman Curls				Exercise #9 Hip Adduction				
Aerobic/ Cardio- vascular Exercise	Type		Duration	Exercise #10 Heel Raises				
				Exercise #11 Alternate Toe Raises				

WEEK THIRTEEN

NOTE: Don't forget your active warmup and static stretching before your workout.

DATE:				DATE:			
FRIDAY Abdominal, Back, Lower Body & Aerobic Workout				**SATURDAY** Upper Body & Aerobic Workout			
	WEIGHT	REPS	SET(S)		WEIGHT	REPS	SET(S)
Exercise #1 Abdominal Curls				Exercise #12 Back Rows			
Exercise #2 Reverse Torso Curls				Exercise #13 Chest Presses			
Exercise #3 Oblique Curls				Exercise #14 Chest Flyes			
Exercise #4 Back Extensions				Exercise #15 Shoulder Presses			
Exercise #5 Modified Squats				Exercise #16 Shoulder Side Raises			
Exercise #6 Wide Stance Squats				Exercise #17 Shoulder Front Raises			
Exercise #7 Lunges (RT & LT)				Exercise #18 Triceps Extensions			
Exercise #8 Hip Abduction				Exercise #19 Alternate Biceps Curls			
Exercise #9 Hip Adduction				Exercise #20 Zottman Curls			
Exercise #10 Heel Raises				Aerobic/ Cardio- vascular Exercise	Type	Duration	
Exercise #11 Alternate Toe Raises							
Aerobic/ Cardio- vascular Exercise	Type	Duration					

WEEK THIRTEEN

NOTE: Don't forget your active warmup and static stretching before your workout.

DATE:				DATE:	DATE:			
SUNDAY Abdominal, Back & Lower Body Workout				MONDAY OFF	**TUESDAY** Abdominal, Back, Lower Body & Aerobic Workout			
	WEIGHT	REPS	SET(S)			WEIGHT	REPS	SET(S)
Exercise #1 Abdominal Curls					Exercise #1 Abdominal Curls			
Exercise #2 Reverse Torso Curls					Exercise #2 Reverse Torso Curls			
Exercise #3 Oblique Curls					Exercise #3 Oblique Curls			
Exercise #4 Back Extensions					Exercise #4 Back Extensions			
Exercise #5 Modified Squats					Exercise #5 Modified Squats			
Exercise #6 Wide Stance Squats					Exercise #6 Wide Stance Squats			
Exercise #7 Lunges (RT & LT)					Exercise #7 Lunges (RT & LT)			
Exercise #8 Hip Abduction					Exercise #8 Hip Abduction			
Exercise #9 Hip Adduction					Exercise #9 Hip Adduction			
Exercise #10 Heel Raises					Exercise #10 Heel Raises			
Exercise #11 Alternate Toe Raises					Exercise #11 Alternate Toe Raises			
					Aerobic/ Cardio- vascular Exercise	Type	Duration	

WEEK FOURTEEN

NOTE: Don't forget your active warmup and static stretching before your workout.

DATE:				DATE:				DATE:
WEDNESDAY Upper Body & Aerobic Workout				**THURSDAY** Abdominal, Back & Lower Body Workout				FRIDAY OFF
	WEIGHT	REPS	SET(S)		WEIGHT	REPS	SET(S)	
Exercise #12 Back Rows				Exercise #1 Abdominal Curls				
Exercise #13 Chest Presses				Exercise #2 Reverse Torso Curls				
Exercise #14 Chest Flyes				Exercise #3 Oblique Curls				
Exercise #15 Shoulder Presses				Exercise #4 Back Extensions				
Exercise #16 Shoulder Side Raises				Exercise #5 Modified Squats				
Exercise #17 Shoulder Front Raises				Exercise #6 Wide Stance Squats				
Exercise #18 Triceps Extensions				Exercise #7 Lunges (RT & LT)				
Exercise #19 Alternate Biceps Curls				Exercise #8 Hip Abduction				
Exercise #20 Zottman Curls				Exercise #9 Hip Adduction				
Aerobic/ Cardio-vascular Exercise	Type		Duration	Exercise #10 Heel Raises				
				Exercise #11 Alternate Toe Raises				

WEEK FOURTEEN

NOTE: Don't forget your active warmup and static stretching before your workout.

DATE:				DATE:			
SATURDAY Abdominal, Back, Lower Body & Aerobic Workout				**SUNDAY** Upper Body & Aerobic Workout			
	WEIGHT	REPS	SET(S)		WEIGHT	REPS	SET(S)
Exercise #1 Abdominal Curls				Exercise #12 Back Rows			
Exercise #2 Reverse Torso Curls				Exercise #13 Chest Presses			
Exercise #3 Oblique Curls				Exercise #14 Chest Flyes			
Exercise #4 Back Extensions				Exercise #15 Shoulder Presses			
Exercise #5 Modified Squats				Exercise #16 Shoulder Side Raises			
Exercise #6 Wide Stance Squats				Exercise #17 Shoulder Front Raises			
Exercise #7 Lunges (RT & LT)				Exercise #18 Triceps Extensions			
Exercise #8 Hip Abduction				Exercise #19 Alternate Biceps Curls			
Exercise #9 Hip Adduction				Exercise #20 Zottman Curls			
Exercise #10 Heel Raises				Aerobic/ Cardio- vascular Exercise	Type		Duration
Exercise #11 Alternate Toe Raises							
Aerobic/ Cardio- vascular Exercise	Type		Duration				

WEEK FIFTEEN

NOTE: Don't forget your active warmup and static stretching before your workout.

DATE:				DATE:	DATE:			
MONDAY Abdominal, Back & Lower Body Workout				TUESDAY OFF	**WEDNESDAY** Abdominal, Back, Lower Body & Aerobic Workout			
	WEIGHT	REPS	SET(S)			WEIGHT	REPS	SET(S)
Exercise #1 Abdominal Curls					Exercise #1 Abdominal Curls			
Exercise #2 Reverse Torso Curls					Exercise #2 Reverse Torso Curls			
Exercise #3 Oblique Curls					Exercise #3 Oblique Curls			
Exercise #4 Back Extensions					Exercise #4 Back Extensions			
Exercise #5 Modified Squats					Exercise #5 Modified Squats			
Exercise #6 Wide Stance Squats					Exercise #6 Wide Stance Squats			
Exercise #7 Lunges (RT & LT)					Exercise #7 Lunges (RT & LT)			
Exercise #8 Hip Abduction					Exercise #8 Hip Abduction			
Exercise #9 Hip Adduction					Exercise #9 Hip Adduction			
Exercise #10 Heel Raises					Exercise #10 Heel Raises			
Exercise #11 Alternate Toe Raises					Exercise #11 Alternate Toe Raises			
					Aerobic/ Cardio-vascular Exercise	Type	Duration	

WEEK FIFTEEN

NOTE: Don't forget your active warmup and static stretching before your workout.

DATE:				DATE:				DATE:
THURSDAY Upper Body & Aerobic Workout				**FRIDAY** Abdominal, Back & Lower Body Workout				SATURDAY OFF
	WEIGHT	REPS	SET(S)		WEIGHT	REPS	SET(S)	
Exercise #12 Back Rows				Exercise #1 Abdominal Curls				
Exercise #13 Chest Presses				Exercise #2 Reverse Torso Curls				
Exercise #14 Chest Flyes				Exercise #3 Oblique Curls				
Exercise #15 Shoulder Presses				Exercise #4 Back Extensions				
Exercise #16 Shoulder Side Raises				Exercise #5 Modified Squats				
Exercise #17 Shoulder Front Raises				Exercise #6 Wide Stance Squats				
Exercise #18 Triceps Extensions				Exercise #7 Lunges (RT & LT)				
Exercise #19 Alternate Biceps Curls				Exercise #8 Hip Abduction				
Exercise #20 Zottman Curls				Exercise #9 Hip Adduction				
Aerobic/ Cardio- vascular Exercise	Type		Duration	Exercise #10 Heel Raises				
				Exercise #11 Alternate Toe Raises				

WEEK SIXTEEN

NOTE: Don't forget your active warmup and static stretching before your workout.

DATE:				DATE:			
SUNDAY Abdominal, Back, Lower Body & Aerobic Workout				**MONDAY** Upper Body & Aerobic Workout			
	WEIGHT	REPS	SET(S)	WEIGHT	REPS	SET(S)	
Exercise #1 Abdominal Curls				Exercise #12 Back Rows			
Exercise #2 Reverse Torso Curls				Exercise #13 Chest Presses			
Exercise #3 Oblique Curls				Exercise #14 Chest Flyes			
Exercise #4 Back Extensions				Exercise #15 Shoulder Presses			
Exercise #5 Modified Squats				Exercise #16 Shoulder Side Raises			
Exercise #6 Wide Stance Squats				Exercise #17 Shoulder Front Raises			
Exercise #7 Lunges (RT & LT)				Exercise #18 Triceps Extensions			
Exercise #8 Hip Abduction				Exercise #19 Alternate Biceps Curls			
Exercise #9 Hip Adduction				Exercise #20 Zottman Curls			
Exercise #10 Heel Raises				Aerobic/ Cardio- vascular Exercise	Type	Duration	
Exercise #11 Alternate Toe Raises							
Aerobic/ Cardio- vascular Exercise	Type	Duration					

WEEK SIXTEEN

NOTE: Don't forget your active warmup and static stretching before your workout.

DATE:				DATE:	DATE:			
TUESDAY Abdominal, Back & Lower Body Workout				WEDNESDAY OFF	**THURSDAY** Abdominal, Back, Lower Body & Aerobic Workout			
	WEIGHT	REPS	SET(S)			WEIGHT	REPS	SET(S)
Exercise #1 Abdominal Curls					Exercise #1 Abdominal Curls			
Exercise #2 Reverse Torso Curls					Exercise #2 Reverse Torso Curls			
Exercise #3 Oblique Curls					Exercise #3 Oblique Curls			
Exercise #4 Back Extensions					Exercise #4 Back Extensions			
Exercise #5 Modified Squats					Exercise #5 Modified Squats			
Exercise #6 Wide Stance Squats					Exercise #6 Wide Stance Squats			
Exercise #7 Lungs (RT & LT)					Exercise #7 Lunges (RT & LT)			
Exercise #8 Hip Abduction					Exercise #8 Hip Abduction			
Exercise #9 Hip Adduction					Exercise #9 Hip Adduction			
Exercise #10 Heel Raises					Exercise #10 Heel Raises			
Exercise #11 Alternate Toe Raises					Exercise #11 Alternate Toe Raises			
					Aerobic/ Cardio- vascular Exercise	Type	Duration	

WEEK SIXTEEN

NOTE: Don't forget your active warmup and static stretching before your workout.

DATE:				DATE:				DATE:
FRIDAY Upper Body & Aerobic Workout				**SATURDAY** Abdominal, Back & Lower Body Workout				SUNDAY OFF
	WEIGHT	REPS	SET(S)		WEIGHT	REPS	SET(S)	
Exercise #12 Back Rows				Exercise #1 Abdominal Curls				
Exercise #13 Chest Presses				Exercise #2 Reverse Torso Curls				
Exercise #14 Chest Flyes				Exercise #3 Oblique Curls				
Exercise #15 Shoulder Presses				Exercise #4 Back Extensions				
Exercise #16 Shoulder Side Raises				Exercise #5 Modified Squats				
Exercise #17 Shoulder Front Raises				Exercise #6 Wide Stance Squats				
Exercise #18 Triceps Extensions				Exercise #7 Lunges (RT & LT)				
Exercise #19 Alternate Biceps Curls				Exercise #8 Hip Abduction				
Exercise #20 Zottman Curls				Exercise #9 Hip Adduction				
Aerobic/ Cardio- vascular Exercise	Type		Duration	Exercise #10 Heel Raises				
				Exercise #11 Alternate Toe Raises				

9
EATING WELL

By now you understand how and why you are going to be burning calories faster than ever on this program. You know you'll be changing the composition of your body by trading your fat for calorie-consuming lean muscle tissue. I've promised you that you're going to lose weight rapidly without dieting.

I'll bet you don't believe me.

But I said this is a no-diet program, and I mean it.

I would be foolish to put you on a diet because, as we all know, diets don't work.

What is a diet, after all? The idea is to eat less so that your body will be forced to burn stored fat for fuel. But eating less sounds a lot easier than it is. Dieting makes you hungry and so cranky that you are ready to strangle your boss, your spouse, even your personal trainer. If you give in to temptation and eat something "bad," you figure you've blown it and give up. You get disgusted with yourself and beat yourself up for lack of willpower.

Not only are diets self-defeating psychologically, they're self-defeating physically. Even people who succeed in losing weight usually regain every single pound plus a few extra.

That's right. Every time you regain lost weight, you end up fatter than you were to start with. There's an easy-to-understand scientific explanation for this.

THE INFAMOUS YO-YO

Researchers have a name for the pattern of putting on extra fat whenever you regain weight you lost by dieting. They call it the "yo-yo" syndrome. It's a vicious cycle that you'll never have to worry about again.

When you go on a diet and lose weight, you also lose lean muscle tissue. As you regain, you put back the fat. But without exercise there's no way to replace your lost lean muscle tissue. The result is that you end up with a lower muscle–fat ratio than you had before your diet. Naturally your metabolism slows down to reflect this change in body composition. You end up fatter than ever.

That can't happen on my program because from day one you'll be burning fat through exercise and building lean muscle tissue. This is going to result in weight loss without dieting and a toned, taut body.

FACT: To lose one pound of fat you have to burn 3,500 calories. It doesn't matter *how* you use up those calories. You can diet and regain, or you can exercise and make a permanent change in your body.

I would never suggest that you go on a diet, because if I did, this would just be another program that doesn't work.

But as your personal trainer, I wouldn't be doing my job if I failed to educate you about eating well.

I want you to treat your new body with respect.

I want you to feel as good as you look.

And I want you to eat good, nutritious food that will enhance your health and increase your energy to better enjoy life.

On this program you're putting a lot of effort into changing your shape. Why not work from the inside out, too?

YOU REALLY ARE WHAT YOU EAT

Our bodies reflect our eating habits in more ways than just their size. Five of the ten leading causes of death in the United States are directly related to our diets: heart disease, cancer, stroke, diabetes, and atherosclerosis (the clogging and hardening of the arteries leading to the heart). Did you know that one out of three Americans will develop a risk factor for heart disease before age sixty, due, in most cases, to poor diet?

You know as well as I do what the problem is.

The biggest culprit in this depressing scenario is all the fat we eat.

WHY FAT MAKES YOU FAT

How much fat is in your daily diet?

If you are typical, the amount adds up to 40 percent or more of all the calories you consume.

FACT: Calorie for calorie, fats are more fattening than other foods. One gram of fat contains 9 calories, compared with 4 calories per gram of protein or carbohydrate.

Not only are fats the most fattening foods, our bodies also *handle* them differently. Did you know that you burn carbohydrate calories *before* you burn up calories from fat? As a result, fat calories are a lot more likely to be stored as body fat. One scientific study showed that if you consumed 100 extra carbohydrate calories, your body would use 23 of them for processing and would store the other 77. But if the 100 extra calories came from fat, only 3 would be burned in processing and 97 would be stored.

Researchers have learned that people today are fatter than they were at the turn of the century. You don't have to look too far for the reason.

FACT: Since 1900 the percentage of calories from fat in the average American diet has increased from 30 percent to well over 40 percent. At the same time, we have become less active physically.

No wonder thirty-four million Americans are obese and have low energy levels.

FATS AND HEALTH

Changing the way you eat can protect you from today's deadliest diseases. In the case of heart disease, researchers have shown that drastically reducing the amount of fat in the diet actually can help unblock coronary arteries clogged with cholesterol. (Heart attacks occur when blood can no longer flow freely to the heart because deposits of cholesterol have narrowed the path through coronary arteries.)

Cholesterol is a fatty substance your body makes on its own and extracts from certain fats in your diet.

224   All fats are fattening, but only one type is associated with artery-clogging cholesterol: the saturated fats found in red meat, dairy products, and other foods from animal sources. The only nonanimal fats that contribute to the artery-clogging process are coconut, cocoa butter, and palm oils used in commercially baked goods.

Saturated fat is easy to recognize: it's always *solid* at room temperature. Think of butter, lard, and chicken fat.

Between 15 and 17 percent of the total calories in the typical American diet comes from saturated fats. In countries where diets are lower in saturated fat, heart disease rates are lower, too. For example, only 7 percent of daily calories consumed by the Japanese are saturated fat—and the Japanese have the lowest rate of heart disease in the world.

The American Heart Association recommends limiting intake of saturated fats to 10 percent of daily calories. That means cutting back on the following foods:

- red meat, particularly "prime"-grade meats, short ribs, spare ribs, and steaks.
- corned beef, pastrami, frankfurters, sausage, bacon, and luncheon meats.
- butter and other fats from animal products (bacon drippings, ham hocks, lard, salt pork)
- gravy made from meat drippings
- whole milk, cream, half-and-half, buttermilk, yogurt made from whole milk, condensed milk, evaporated milk, and ice cream
- cheeses
- cream sauces and cream soups

Other types of fat aren't as bad for your heart and general health as saturated fats, but they're just as fattening. Your body processes and stores them the same way it deals with saturated fats.

The two other types of fat are monounsaturates and polyunsaturates. Both come from plants, and neither contains cholesterol or contributes to high cholesterol levels in the body.

Olive and canola oils are monounsaturates. Corn, safflower, sunflower, soybean, and cottonseed oils are polyunsaturates. You're most likely to consume these fats in salad dressings and as part of cooked foods, particularly fried foods.

While monounsaturates and polyunsaturates have not been linked to specific diseases, the fact that they are fats means that they contribute to obesity and to all of the health problems associated with being overweight and eating a high-fat diet. These include high blood pressure, diabetes, and breast, prostate, endometrial, ovarian, and colon cancer.

Just limiting fat consumption can speed your weight loss on this program. For example, if you typically consume 2,000 calories a day and 40 percent of those calories come from fat, by cutting the fat in half, you would eliminate 400 calories a day. Over the course of this sixteen-week program that would add up to *44,800* calories and translate into a thirteen-pound fat loss *in addition* to the fat you are going to burn off with exercise.

So how could you cut out 400 fat calories?

Let me count the ways.

I'd better not catch you eating too many fatty foods!

You could save 50 calories (per glass) by switching from whole milk to 1 percent milk.

You could save 178 calories by having a Fudgsicle instead of a scoop of vanilla ice cream. (You would save 258 calories if you switch from an extra-creamy premium-brand ice cream to a Fudgsicle.)

You could save 60 calories by having an English muffin instead of a doughnut.

Switch from granola to cornflakes and you save 250 calories per half-cup serving!

You can save about 100 calories (and get more to eat) by substituting 1 cup of popcorn for 1 ounce of corn chips or potato chips.

You can save 130 calories by substituting ten small stick pretzels for 1 ounce of potato chips.

You can save more than 100 calories by substituting a baked potato *with* a teaspoon of butter for a typical restaurant serving of French fries.

You can save 115 calories by substituting 8 ounces of roast chicken *with* the skin for an 8-ounce burger (meat only). *You save another 100 calories by removing the chicken skin!*

Have a turkey sandwich (7 ounces of meat) instead of an 8-ounce burger and save 350 calories.

Those savings add up to more than 1,400 calories without dieting!

CONNIE GRECO

Algonquin, Illinois

Connie Greco has written me twice. Before she started exercising, her body actually hurt when she moved. She could walk up the stairs only by holding on to the railing and pulling herself up. Now she can actually run up. Connie has lost thirty-two pounds and approximately thirty-three inches. She hasn't reached her goal yet, but she's well on her way. And she feels better than ever physically and mentally:

"I've been losing inches, and my energy level has increased along with my self-esteem. As I have continued to lose, I've begun to like my body more and more, and the more I like my body, the better care I take of it. I work out six days a week.

"Not only are inches melting away, but my body is shaping up. I look almost the same as I did when I weighed thirty pounds less than I do now. I eat anything I want, and I haven't gained one ounce since I've been exercising."

Connie is so excited about her progress that she wants everyone to know, particularly "the people hurting from the pain of being obese. I want to show them that the miracle we've all been looking for is right here for the asking."

What do you think of that? Connie really has changed her life!

CARBOHYDRATES

The more fruits, vegetables, and grains you eat, the better. I love this because it allows me to eat pasta, pasta, and more pasta.

Plant foods of almost every description qualify as carbohydrates. With the exception of olives, avocados, and nuts, all carbohydrates are fat-free. They're also loaded with vitamins.

There are two types of carbohydrates, simple and complex. Simple carbohydrates are sugars and other sweets. These are the so-called empty calories because they have no nutritional value. The less of them you eat, the better.

On the other hand, complex carbohydrates, including such starches as breads and pasta, are the best foods you can eat and should add up to between 40 and 60 percent of your daily calories.

Most veteran dieters are shocked at the idea of eating so many starchy foods. But in fact, carbohydrates are less fattening than other types of food. What makes them fattening are the fats we add to them: butter on baked potatoes, cream or cheese sauces on pasta.

The more fat-free carbohydrates in your diet, the fewer calories you'll consume and the more quickly you will lose fat. Emphasizing complex carbohydrates is also the healthiest way to eat, particularly when your diet includes foods that are high in fiber.

Fiber

Fiber, a component of plant foods, is the undigestible residue of grains, fruits, and vegetables. High-fiber diets are associated with a low risk of cancer. As a matter of fact, the American Health Foundation estimates that 75 percent of colon cancer and 50 percent of breast cancer could be prevented by reducing fat consumption and increasing the amount of fiber in the diet. So do the fiber gig, okay?

Fiber functions as a natural "internal broom" that sweeps through our intestines, moving food along quickly and easily. By softening foods, adding bulk, and attracting water to our stools, it prevents constipation, relieves hemorrhoid symptoms, and seems to protect against colon and rectal cancers.

The only drawback to adding fiber to your diet is that a sudden increase can cause bloating and intestinal gas. This usually is a temporary problem and may not develop at all if you gradually increase the amount of fiber you consume.

228   PROTEIN

Most people think they need a lot more protein than they really do. We couldn't survive without protein—it provides us with essential amino acids needed for good health. But we need surprisingly little. The Recommended Dietary Allowance (RDA) for men is only 56 grams of protein, about 2 ounces. Women need only 44 grams daily, about 1½ ounces. It doesn't matter whether the protein you eat comes from meats or other animal sources (including dairy products) or from combining vegetable sources of protein like legumes (peas, lentils, chick peas) with rice and other grains. The difference between animal and vegetable sources of protein is that animal products offer chemically complete protein. To get complete protein from plant sources, you have to know how to combine certain foods properly. A vegetarian diet may not appeal to you (I'm not recommending it), but you should know that it can be as healthy as—if not more healthy than—nonvegetarian eating. (If you decide to try a vegetarian diet, be sure to take a supplement of vitamin B_{12}, particularly if you eliminate eggs and dairy products.)

THE FOOD PYRAMID

So what is a healthy diet?

We now know that a healthy diet is high in carbohydrates like bread, cereal, rice, and pasta. All of these foods are fat-free (unless you add butter, cheese, or rich sauces). Guidelines for a healthy diet suggest that we model our food choices on the food pyramid illustrated on the next page. As you can see, the foods at the base of the pyramid are the breads, cereals, rice, and pasta that should make up the bulk of your diet, between six and eleven servings per day.

Next come fruits and vegetables: two to four servings of fruit and three to five servings of vegetables.

Next come dairy products, including milk, yogurt, and cheese (two to three servings), and meat, poultry, fish, eggs, dry beans, and nuts (two to three servings).

And at the tip of the pyramid are fats, oils, and sweets, to be eaten sparingly.

My only quarrel with the food pyramid is the word *sparingly*. What does that mean? How many calories does it add up to? My suggestion is that you follow the recommendation of the American Heart Association and keep your intake of fats and oils to 30 percent *or less* of your daily intake of calories. I personally try to keep my fat consumption below 25 percent of total calories. On page 240 you're going to calculate how many calories per day to eat to get the full benefit of this program. If your total comes to, say, 1,600 calories per day, 30 percent would amount to 480 calories per day; 25 percent would allow you 400 calories from fat out of a 1,600-calorie total.

Food Guide Pyramid

A Guide to Daily Food Choices

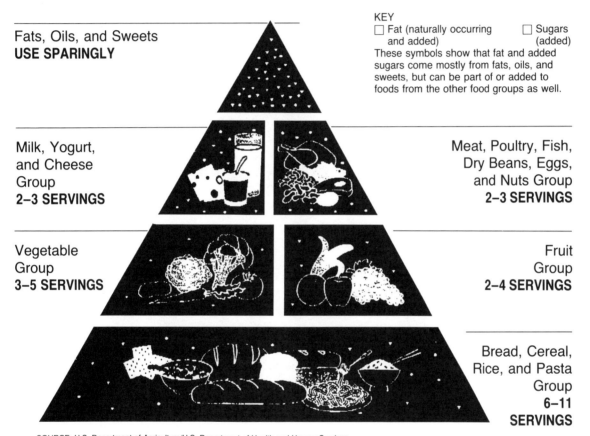

Fats, Oils, and Sweets
USE SPARINGLY

KEY
☐ Fat (naturally occurring   ☐ Sugars
  and added)   (added)
These symbols show that fat and added
sugars come mostly from fats, oils, and
sweets, but can be part of or added to
foods from the other food groups as well.

Milk, Yogurt,
and Cheese
Group
2–3 SERVINGS

Meat, Poultry, Fish,
Dry Beans, Eggs,
and Nuts Group
2–3 SERVINGS

Vegetable
Group
3–5 SERVINGS

Fruit
Group
2–4 SERVINGS

Bread, Cereal,
Rice, and Pasta
Group
**6–11
SERVINGS**

SOURCE: U.S. Department of Agriculture/U.S. Department of Health and Human Services

1153 cal

SERVINGS

What's your idea of a "serving"?

   The folks who designed the food pyramid had very specific amounts for each type of food:

Breads, Cereals, Rice, and Pasta

One serving equals

- 1 slice of bread (or 1 ounce of bread)
- ½ cup cooked rice or pasta
- ½ cup cooked cereal
- 1 ounce of ready-to-eat cereal

Vegetables

One serving equals

- ½ cup chopped, raw, or cooked veggies
- 1 cup of leafy raw vegetables

Fruits

One serving equals

- 1 piece of fruit or melon wedge
- ¾ cup of juice
- ½ cup of canned fruit
- ¼ cup of dried fruit

Milk, Yogurt, Cheese

One serving equals

- 1 cup of milk or yogurt
- 1½–2 ounces of cheese

Meat, Poultry, Fish, Dry Beans

One serving equals

- 2½–3 ounces of cooked lean meat, poultry, or fish
- 1 egg, ½ cup cooked beans, or 2 tablespoons of peanut butter count as 1 ounce of lean meat (about ⅓ serving)

What is a fat or oil serving? Except for butter or margarine, we don't actually see the fat we use. Most of it is mixed into salad dressings or used in cooking. But you can get an approximation of the amount you use daily. Just remember that 1 tablespoon of butter, margarine, or oil contains about 100 calories. Read food labels carefully to find out how much fat is present.

READING LABELS

The key item of information on product labels is the fat content. In the past you had to calculate how many fat calories a packaged food contained by multiplying grams of fat listed by nine (the number of calories per gram of fat). Luckily, new government-developed labels introduced in 1994 make it a lot easier to know what you're getting when you buy packaged foods.

First of all, the government has developed specific standards a food must meet before it can be labeled "healthy." From now on, "healthy" means that the food contains no more than 60 milligrams of cholesterol, 3 grams of fat, and 1 gram of saturated fat per serving. To be considered "healthy," a food also must provide at least 10 percent of our daily needs for vitamin A, vitamin C, iron, calcium, protein, or fiber. Sodium limits will be phased in by 1998. At that time, to qualify for a "healthy" label, sodium content must not exceed 360 milligrams for individual foods and 480 milligrams for packaged meals.

The new labels list total calories per serving and the number of calories derived from fat. Farther down on the label is a breakdown of the types of fat the food contains (saturated, polyunsaturated, monounsaturated), as well as the amounts of cholesterol, sodium, fiber, vitamins, calcium, and iron per serving.

The number of calories from fat is still all-important because it'll help you determine whether the food is low enough in fat to keep your consumption below 30 percent of daily calories.

The percent of daily calories from fat listed on the new labels is based on a diet of 2,000 calories per day. This sounds more confusing than it is. If you're trying to keep fat calories down to 30 percent of daily calories and you typically eat 2,000 calories per day, you can consume 600 calories' worth of fat. Therefore, if a food contains 60 calories from fat, the label will state that it provides 10 percent of fat calories for the day. If you're trying to keep your fat calories below 600 per day, you'll have to do some math to figure out how much of your personal total a given food provides. For example, if you want to limit fat to no more than 400 calories per day, a food with 60 calories from fat will provide you with 15 percent of your daily limit. Just divide the number of fat calories listed on the label by the daily limit you have set for yourself.

SODIUM

If you have high blood pressure or retain water easily after consuming foods high in sodium (a component of salt), be sure to check the sodium content on food labels. You also may be surprised to learn that in some areas tapwater is very high in sodium.

Average salt intake is between 4 and 6 grams daily, much more than the 1.1 to 3.3 grams considered adequate for good health. Most of the salt in our diets comes from processed and commercially prepared foods. Canned vegetables and soups usually are high in sodium.

Just cutting down on salt can knock off a few pounds very quickly. Of course, you're not really losing fat; you're just flushing excess water out of your system. But if you're a salt lover, you would be surprised at how much extra water you are lugging around inside you. Get rid of it and your clothes will be looser within days.

To reduce your salt consumption, always taste the food on your plate before adding salt, and look for foods described as low sodium (less than 140 milligrams per serving), very low sodium (less than 35 milligrams per serving), or sodium-free (less than 5 milligrams per serving). If the label says "unsalted," "no salt added," or "without added salt," the product contains no sodium other than amounts naturally found in the food. The table below lists foods that are high in sodium.

FOODS HIGH IN SODIUM

- dehydrated soup, sauce, and salad dressing mixes
- some ready-to-eat cereals
- most frozen dinners and other convenience foods
- soy sauce
- ketchup
- worcestershire sauce
- pickles and relishes
- mustard, chili sauce
- olives
- processed cheeses and cheese spreads
- baking powder, baking soda
- monosodium glutamate
- any food additive containing the word *sodium*
- canned and/or frozen vegetables in sauce
- hot dogs, sausages, ham, luncheon meats, and canned meats and poultry
- prepared salad dressings
- salted nuts, potato chips, pretzels, corn chips, and other snack foods

CALCIUM

The calcium question is important for everyone. New research shows that this essential mineral is more vital to good health than doctors suspected. We need it for strong teeth and bones, but it also seems to play an important role in keeping blood pressure under control and in protecting against colon cancer.

Unfortunately, most adults, particularly adult women, don't get anywhere near the amount of calcium they need. Experts now believe that the optimal amount of calcium for everyone over the age of eleven is 1,600 milligrams per day, roughly the amount found in five glasses of milk.

The table below lists the foods that are highest in calcium. In addition, some breakfast cereals, fruit juices, and breads are fortified with calcium. Check the labels.

GOOD SOURCES OF CALCIUM

	Mg Calcium
Whole milk, 8 oz.	288
1% milk, 8 oz.	300
Skim milk, 8 oz.	302
Fat-free plain yogurt, 8 oz.	452
Low-fat plain yogurt, 8 oz.	415
Low-fat yogurt with fruit	314
American cheese, 1 oz.	124
Cheddar cheese, 1 oz.	204
Cottage cheese, 1 oz., low fat	138
Mozzarella cheese, part skim	147
Parmesan cheese, grated, 1 tsp.	69
Vanilla ice cream, 1 cup	176
Orange sherbet, 1 cup	103
Ice milk, vanilla, 1 cup	176
Ice milk, vanilla, soft serve, 1 cup	274
Sardines, including bones, 4 canned	184
Broccoli, 1 cup cooked	174
Broccoli, frozen, 1 cup cooked	94
Turnip greens, 1 cup cooked	198
Collards, 1 cup cooked	148
Tofu, 1 cup	260

ALCOHOL

I'm not going to tell you not to drink because I enjoy a glass of wine with meals myself, particularly if it is a great red. But too much, even of a good thing, can be unhealthy and fattening.

We all know the risks of excessive drinking. Not only can it destroy your liver, but if you're a woman and drink too much while pregnant, you put your baby at risk of birth defects.

On the other hand, moderate drinking may be good for us. A number of studies have shown that a daily drink or two reduces the risk of heart disease.

But there is no denying the fact that alcohol is high in calories and low in nutrients. Even worse, your body will burn calories from alcohol before it burns anything else.

My message on the subject of alcohol can be summed up in one word: moderation.

WATER

As your personal trainer, I definitely recommend that you drink eight 8-ounce glasses of water daily.

You will find you need to drink a lot of water to replenish fluids lost during and after exercise. Water is the best liquid for avoiding dehydration. It also cleanses your body, helps flush impurities out of your system, and regulates your body temperature.

I prefer a good mineral water, plain or carbonated, to regular tapwater. To reduce water retention, drink distilled water.

VITAMIN AND MINERAL SUPPLEMENTS

If you follow the nutritional guidelines in this chapter, you'll be getting all the vitamins and minerals needed for good health. If not, I recommend taking a good multi-vitamin/mineral supplement for a healthy, high-energy life. I also believe that amino acid complex can help athletes keep metabolism high and muscle growth stimulated. To find the combination best for you, go to a good health food store and consult with an expert on your individual needs.

CHARLES TOLES

Cicero, New York

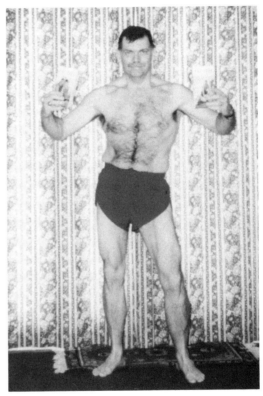

That's Charles Toles before and after my workout program. He was a big baby, a fat kid, and even a fat marine. "Over the years I tried everything," he wrote. "I got fast small results and then regained the weight and then some." Even the marines didn't help. "They put me in the conditioning platoon, otherwise known as the Fat Farm, where they starve and work you to the bone but don't teach or help you try to keep the weight off."

In September 1993 Charles's doctor advised him to lose sixty pounds. Not long after that he saw me on television and was inspired by the testimonials "from other people like myself" to say 'Why not me?'

"Between your program and a little research into fats and calories, I've been able to win the battle of the bulge. Now foods I once thought were terrible have taken on a different flavor. And high-fat foods like pizza and Oreos taste different and make me uncomfortable. I can even eat in restaurants without compromising my low-fat style: I just bring my own salad dressing."

Results? In a little over five months Charles lost ninety pounds and brought his cholesterol level down to normal.

"This is not a diet. It's a life-style change," he wrote.

I couldn't have said it better myself.

236 EATING IN RESTAURANTS

I eat three meals a day in restaurants. I have for years. And I don't have any trouble at all getting exactly the healthy foods I want.

I just ask for them.

At one of my favorite Italian restaurants, the waitress knows what I'm going to order when I walk in the door. She doesn't even hand me a menu. She'll just ask if I want the regular: a plate of plain pasta with marinara sauce on the side.

I learned a long time ago that the secret to eating well on the road is to make up my mind beforehand exactly what I want. I don't look at the menu. I just make my request.

And I almost always get it.

You are paying for your meal, so why shouldn't you have it your way?

I admit that getting exactly what you want can be tough in fast-food restaurants, where the kitchen is no more than a microwave and no one really cooks. For that reason, I avoid fast-food places whenever possible. Although many now have added salad bars and low-fat specials, most of the food is still very high in fat.

FACTS: A Big Mac contains 570 calories, 315 of them (55 percent) from fat.

A Whopper contains 640 calories, 369 of them (58 percent) from fat.

A Wendy's Hot Stuffed Baked Potato with Bacon and Cheese contains 570 calories, 270 of them (47 percent) from fat.

Yuck.

Here are some hints to help you get what you want in restaurants:

- Select restaurants that cook food on the premises. The better the restaurant, the more willing the kitchen will be to do it your way.
- Become a "regular" diner at a restaurant you like. Once you become a familiar face to the waiters, the owner, or the maître d', the staff will be happy to accommodate your request and treat you like royalty when you arrive.
- Stick to fish and chicken. Save beef for home consumption unless you're eating at a very high quality restaurant.
- Ask for sauces and salad dressings—everything—on the side.
- Order meats, poultry, or fish baked, broiled, or poached instead of fried or sautéed.
- At breakfast request that your toast, muffin, or bagel be served unbuttered. Add the butter yourself or, better yet, substitute jam for butter. A tablespoon of strawberry jam contains 55 calories and no fat, compared to butter with 100 calories, all of them from fat.
- Watch out for words that mean the dish has been cooked in or with fat (sauté, tempura, au gratin, fried, pan-fried, crispy, creamed, in cream sauce, hollandaise, Parmesan, escalloped, stewed, basted, buttery, buttered).

- Never be shy about asking for what you want. Remember who's paying the check and forking over the tip.

KEEPING TRACK

Before you try to change your eating habits, find out exactly what you do eat on a few typical days. How else are you going to figure out where to cut the fat? Use the chart on page 238 to keep track. Write down *everything* you eat—meals, snacks, and tastings of food while you prepare meals. Be as specific as possible about amounts.

Keeping this log will help you in two ways.

- It'll show you exactly what and how much you are eating.
- It'll give you a starting point from which to cut fat calories.

I've included extra logs on pages 238 and 239 for you to use as you begin to make changes in your eating habits. There are spaces to note the fat content of the foods you eat. If you need more space, make extra copies of the logs.

Writing things down will help you lose weight because it will make you aware of what and how much you eat. It also will help to reinforce changes in eating patterns.

LET ME HOLD YOUR HAND

On the following pages you'll find specific nutritional guidelines to help you make healthy changes in your eating habits. Remember, these are guidelines, not a diet. But if you need ideas for healthy food choices, the suggested menus will give you an idea of how to plan meals and make food selections.

HOW MUCH SHOULD YOU EAT?

I'll bet you don't believe you can lose serious weight just by cutting down on the fats in your diet. If you try it, you'll see that I am right, but if you're a planner and want to know how much you can eat and still lose weight (or stay the same or gain), I can help.

There's a formula that lets you figure out exactly how many calories you can consume at your exercise level and lose, maintain, or gain.

CONCEIVE! BELIEVE! ACHIEVE!
"You Are What You Eat"

DATE:						
	BREAKFAST	SNACK	LUNCH	SNACK	DINNER	SNACK
PROTEIN						
GRAIN						
VEGETABLE						
FRUIT						
DAIRY						
FAT						

DATE:						
	BREAKFAST	SNACK	LUNCH	SNACK	DINNER	SNACK
PROTEIN						
GRAIN						
VEGETABLE						
FRUIT						
DAIRY						
FAT						

DATE:						
	BREAKFAST	SNACK	LUNCH	SNACK	DINNER	SNACK
PROTEIN						
GRAIN						
VEGETABLE						
FRUIT						
DAIRY						
FAT						

CONCEIVE! BELIEVE! ACHIEVE!
"You Are What You Eat"

DATE:						
	BREAKFAST	SNACK	LUNCH	SNACK	DINNER	SNACK
PROTEIN						
GRAIN						
VEGETABLE						
FRUIT						
DAIRY						
FAT						

DATE:						
	BREAKFAST	SNACK	LUNCH	SNACK	DINNER	SNACK
PROTEIN						
GRAIN						
VEGETABLE						
FRUIT						
DAIRY						
FAT						

DATE:						
	BREAKFAST	SNACK	LUNCH	SNACK	DINNER	SNACK
PROTEIN						
GRAIN						
VEGETABLE						
FRUIT						
DAIRY						
FAT						

240

Get out your calculator. If you want exact information, you will now have to do some math. Write down your results step by step in the space provided below.

To start your calculation you'll need two figures:

- Your weight: __132__ 140
- Your body fat percentage (from caliper measurements or the calculation of body mass index on page 35) __24__ 24

With these two numbers you can calculate your lean body mass. (For an example of the calculation, see page 241).

First, multiply your body fat percentage (F) by your weight (W) as follows:

1. (W) _____ × (F) _____ = _____ (#1)
   Now, subtract the result of #1. from your weight:
2. (W) _____ − (#1) _____ = _____
3. Multiply the result by one of the following figures:
   - *14* if you're exercising at the beginner level
   - *16* if you're exercising at the intermediate level
   - *18* if you're at the advanced level
4. _____ × _____ = _____*

The result above is the number of calories you can consume if you want to maintain your weight.

If you want to lose, subtract 300 from that result.

_____ − 300 = _____ calories per day.

If you want to gain, add 200 to (*)

_____ + 200 = _____ calories per day.

Now you know how many calories you can consume daily. To find out what you can eat at that calorie level, choose the nutritional plan that corresponds to the number of calories you need to lose, maintain, or gain. Then consult the chart on page 241. You will also find sample menus for each plan in appendix 2.

Plan A: 1,200–1,350 calories
Plan B: 1,350–1,650 calories
Plan C: 1,650–2,000 calories
Plan D: 2,000–2,350 calories
Plan E: 2,350–2,500 calories

For information about serving sizes, turn back to page 230.

FOOD GROUP SERVINGS ALLOWED DAILY PER NUTRITIONAL PLAN

	A	B	C	D	E
Grains	6	8	9	11	12
Fruit	2	3	4	5	6
Protein	2	2	2	3	4
Vegetables	3	5	5	6	7
Fat	1	1	2	2	3
Dairy	2	2	3	3	3

For information about serving sizes, turn back to page 230.

EXAMPLE OF THE CALORIE LEVEL COMPUTATION

In this example, I'm using a 160-pound woman whose body fat percentage is 27 percent and who is exercising at the beginner's level.

To find lean body mass:

Multiply her weight (160) by her body fat percentage (.27): $160 \times .27 = 43.2$

Now subtract 43 (rounded off from 43.2) from her weight (160):

$160 - 43 = 117$

117 = lean body mass

To find her calorie level, multiply lean body mass (117) by 14 (the correct figure for those at the beginning workout level)

$117 \times 14 = 1,638$

If this woman wanted to maintain her weight, she would consume roughly 1,600 calories per day.

But if she wanted to lose, she would subtract 300 calories from her total:

$1638 - 300 = 1,338$

For 1,338 calories per day, use Nutrition Plan A

MOST FREQUENTLY ASKED QUESTIONS

1. *What's the difference between muscular strength and muscular endurance?*

   Muscular strength refers to how much resistance a muscle or muscle group can overcome (the amount of weight you can lift). Muscle endurance refers to the ability to repeatedly lift a certain weight or overcome a certain amount of resistance (the number of times you can lift something).

2. *Does stretching improve flexibility?*

   Yes. The static stretches (when you hold a stretch and don't bounce) recommended in this book are great for increasing flexibility when held for ten counts or longer.

3. *What type of aerobic/cardiovascular exercise is best for me?*

   All of the exercises described in this book (see chapter 6) are safe and effective for everyone. If you're very heavy, start out on a stationary or recumbent bike (recumbent is best) or with the brisk walking program.

4. *What type of exercise burns the most fat?*

   During exercise, aerobic/cardiovascular exercise of low intensity and long duration. Resistance exercise burns the most fat *after* the workout because the muscle tissue is metabolically active.

5. *If I don't change my eating habits, will I lose weight by exercising?*

   Yes, provided that you do not eat more than you do now. Your loss will depend on the balance between how many calories you consume and how many you burn daily. And proper exercise technique.

6. *When during exercise should I take my heart rate?*

   Just after your warm-up and just before your cooldown.

7. *Once I reach my goal, how do I maintain my weight and shape?*

   Continue with this program. Work out at least three days per week and cut back on calories and increase exercise *immediately* if your clothes begin to get tight or your measurements increase.

8. *How can I prevent low back problems?*

   Use proper technique when lifting or reaching for objects and maintain good abdominal and back strength as well as hamstring and back flexibility.

9. *How can I kick bad habits?*

Replace bad habits with good ones. Record what you do, when you do it, where you do it, and how you feel when you do it so that you can break the sequence of events associated with feelings that trigger your bad habits.

10. *Why do I need to consult a physician before beginning an exercise program?*

To make sure you have no health problems that may need to be addressed first. You don't want to kick the bucket before you save yourself!

11. *What are amino acids, and why are they important?*

Amino acids are proteins broken down into their simplest form. They're very important because they help build tissue in the body. And, as we've seen, muscle tissue adds shape and contour to the body.

12. *Is breakfast a must?*

Yes. Your blood sugar is low in the morning because you haven't eaten for eight to twelve hours. Breakfast furnishes your body with the fuel you will need during the early part of the day.

13. *How do I eat healthy meals when I don't have time to shop or cook?*

Plan ahead. You have to eat, so think about it beforehand so that you can arrange for healthy, nutritious meals. And it's not so hard to find a local deli!

14. *How can I lose weight but keep up my energy?*

Through sensible eating (low fat) and a well-rounded fitness program. Take a daily multivitamin supplement and make sure you get plenty of rest.

15. *How can I gain weight?*

Eat more calories than you expend. Make sure the additional calories come from complex carbohydrates (see chapter 9). Also 5 to 6 small meals a day are more effective than 3 big ones, especially when complimented by a weight-training program.

16. *How does exercise affect menstruation?*

Intensive training can result in a drop in a woman's body fat percentage below levels at which her reproductive hormones continue to function normally. As a result, menstruation may stop. It should resume once body fat returns to a healthy range (above 17 percent of total body weight).

17. *At what age can a child start exercising?*

Youngsters should not exercise with weight until after age fifteen. However, children can engage in aerobic/cardiovascular exercise, although most will find it pretty boring. Encouraging children to engage in sports from an early age is the best way to ensure that they get lots of healthy exercise.

18. *Should I heat or ice an injury?*

Remember this first-aid acronym: RICE. It stands for rest, *ice,* compression, and elevation. Don't use heat; it tends to increase inflammation.

19. *I have flabby skin as a result of dieting. Will exercise help?*

Absolutely. The progressive resistance exercises described in this book will increase muscle mass and help eliminate flab. The exercise program that we teach in this book is exactly what you're looking for. Just take a look at the before and after pictures.

20. *How do I get off a plateau?*

Change your workout. Vary the duration and intensity of your workout and change the exercise. Keep challenging yourself!

21. *I'm not seeing results. What am I doing wrong?*

   Check to make sure that you're eating as recommended for your goal. Vary your exercise program: try a different type of aerobic/cardiovascular exercise. See my answer to question 20, above. Or write me or my trainers a letter.

22. *Is it okay to break one-half hour of aerobic/cardiovascular exercise into three ten-minute sessions?*

   No. Aerobic/cardiovascular exercise always should be continuous, never intermittent.

23. *Can I exercise to lose in certain areas?*

   Fat loss occurs throughout the body. However, you can spot tone and firm specific areas.

24. *How often to I need to cross-train?*

   Do a different aerobic/cardiovascular exercise at least once a week. The more variety you can manage, the better. Alternate between two or more types of exercise. Cross-training prevents fat loss from plateauing.

25. *Can I do muscle toning every day?*

   Yes, if you work at low intensity. If you use weights, do upper body one day and lower the next. Or do resistance exercises that require pushing one day and pulling the next.

26. *Can I do aerobic/cardiovascular exercise every day?*

   No. You'll get burned out and bored. Three to five days a week is ideal.

27. *Can I do aerobic and weight training on the same day?*

   Yes. But first you need to establish a good level of fitness.

28. *Should I eat before or after exercise?*

   Never work out on an empty stomach or less than an hour after eating.

29. *Which is worse, sugar or fat?*

   Both can be bad for your health, but fat is the biggest enemy. Sugar can rot your teeth and provide you with nutritionally "empty" calories. If you have a sweet tooth, stick to artificially sweetened low-fat desserts, except for the occasional treat. Eventually sugar in the form of excess calories turns into fat.

30. *How often do I need to exercise to maintain?*

   At least three days a week.

31. *Should I lose weight before starting an exercise program?*

   No. If you have a lot of weight to lose and do not do some type of resistance exercise, you'll end up with a lot of sagging skin.

32. *Which is better, free weights or machines?*

   Machines are safer when you're exercising without supervision. Free weights can be better adapted to your range of motion and body size, but you should never use heavy weights except in the presence of a trainer or "spotter."

THE LAST WORD

I've told you everything I can about this one-on-one training program and how and why it can help you transform your body, your energy, and your attitude. Now it's up to you.

But I wouldn't want to leave you without one last demonstration of how well this program works. So take a look at the pictures and captions on the following pages. All of those people made incredible changes in their bodies using the same exercises and the same nutrition plan I have described in this book.

They got the results they wanted.

You will, too.

You can do it.

So do it! NOW!

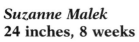

Lynn Marie Carty
23 inches, 11 weeks

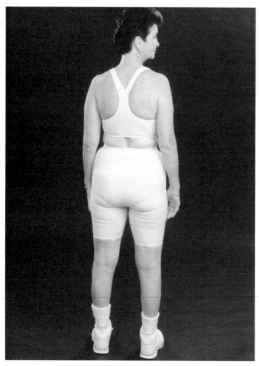

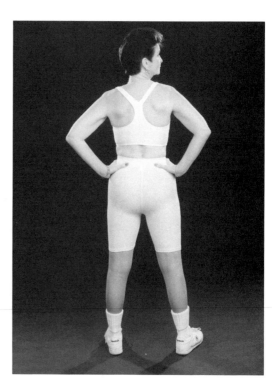

Suzanne Malek
24 inches, 8 weeks

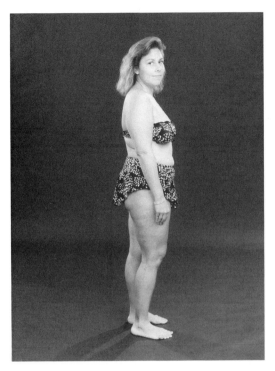

Laura Lothridge
30 inches, 11 weeks

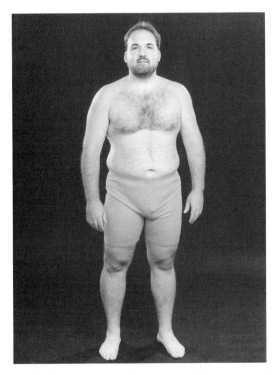
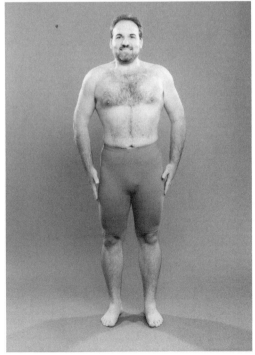

Kevin Lothridge **30 pounds, 11 weeks   another 8 pounds 3 weeks later
totalling 38 pounds in 14 weeks**

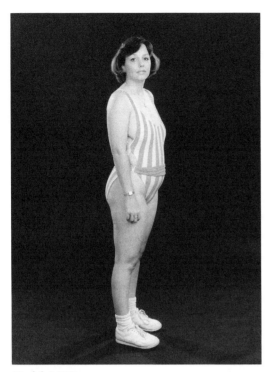 

Debbi Mirra
21 inches, 11 weeks

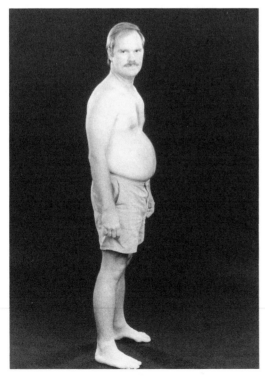 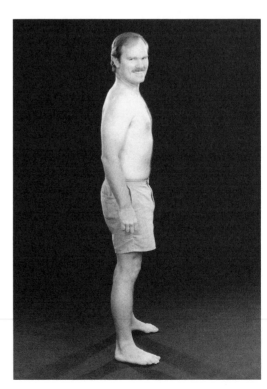

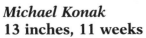
13 inches, 11 weeks

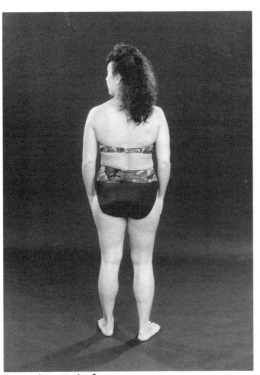

Louise Friedman
32 inches, 6 dress sizes in 11 weeks

Kerry Clem
24 inches, 11 weeks

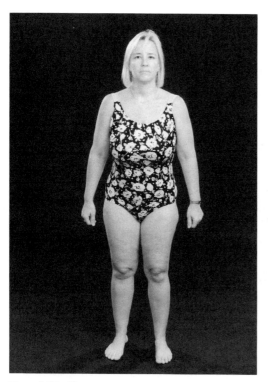

Tami Bails
20 inches, 11 weeks

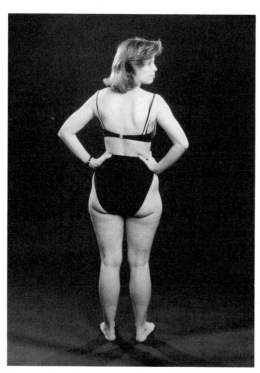

Sherry Sacino
22 inches, 6 weeks   4 more inches in 9 weeks, totalling 26 inches

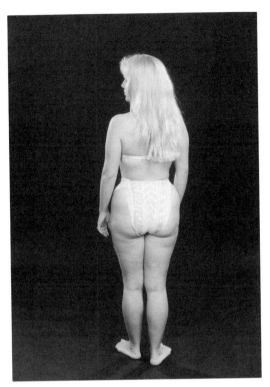 

Jeanne Marie Earley
35 inches, 14 weeks
From a size 12 to size 4

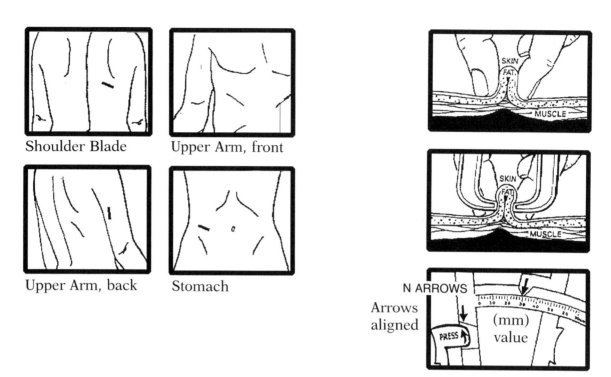

Shoulder Blade

Upper Arm, front

Upper Arm, back

Stomach

N ARROWS

Arrows
aligned

(mm)
value

PRESS

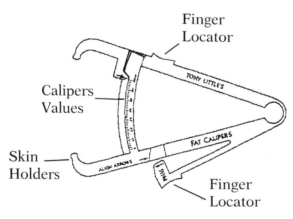

Finger
Locator

Calipers
Values

Skin
Holders

Finger
Locator

	1	2	3	AVG.
Shoulder blade				
Upper arm, front				
Upper arm, back				
Stomach				
Total of averages				

Average body fat percentage = ____

Appendix 1
USING FAT CALIPERS

A fat calipers is a device to help you determine what percentage of your weight comes from fat. It measures a fold of skin and its underlying layers of fat. For the most accurate result, you need to take four separate measurements:

- on your back below the shoulder blade
- on your upper arm over the biceps muscle
- on the back of your upper arm over the triceps muscle
- on your stomach just below your waist

The diagrams on page 254 show exactly where to take the measurements. You'll need someone to help you with the first three. If you can't get help, just take the stomach measurement.

Take your measurements on bare skin while standing up. You'll get the most exact result if you take each measurement three times and average the results. Record your measurements on the chart on page 254.

To take the measurement, first pinch your skin between your thumb and forefinger and pull it away from the muscle as shown in the diagram on page 254.

Place the pincers of the calipers over the midpoint of the skin fold, as shown in the diagram on page 254. Hold the skin fold and press the calipers until the arrows line up as shown in the diagram. Record the result.

Once you've taken all your measurements and recorded them on the chart on page 254, calculate the average measurement for each body site by adding all three measurements and dividing by three. Record the result in the "average" column for that body site.

Total the averages for each body site and record the result in the total column. (If you're only using your stomach measurement, record the average in the total column.)

Referring to the charts on pages 256–258, look down the first column until you find your average calipers value (or stomach calipers value).

Find your age in the top row of the chart.

Locate the point in the chart where your average calipers total (or stomach calipers total) intersect. This is your average body fat percentage. Enter it on the chart on page 254.

% FAT for SUM OF MEASUREMENTS
AT ALL FOUR LOCATIONS—MALE

SUM OF SKINFOLD MEASUREMENTS (mm)	AGE 16–29	AGE 30–39	AGE 40–49	AGE 50+
16	6.7	9.3	9.5	9.7
18	7.9	10.8	10.9	11.0
20	8.1	12.0	12.2	12.5
22	9.2	13.0	13.5	13.9
24	10.2	13.9	14.6	15.1
26	11.2	14.7	15.7	16.3
28	12.1	15.5	16.7	17.4
30	12.9	16.2	17.6	18.5
35	14.7	17.8	19.7	20.8
40	16.3	19.2	21.5	22.8
45	17.2	20.4	23.1	24.7
50	19.0	21.5	24.6	26.3
55	20.2	22.5	25.9	27.8
60	21.2	23.5	27.1	29.1
65	22.2	24.3	28.2	30.4
70	23.2	25.1	29.3	31.5
75	24.0	25.9	30.2	32.6
80	24.8	26.6	31.2	33.7
85	25.6	27.6	32.1	34.6
90	26.3	28.3	32.9	35.5
95	27.0	29.0	33.8	36.5
100	27.6	29.7	34.5	37.3
110	28.8	30.9	35.8	38.8
120	29.9	32.0	37.1	40.2
130	31.0	33.0	38.2	41.5
140	31.9	34.0	39.4	42.8
150	32.8	34.8	40.4	41.9
160	33.6	35.7	41.4	45.0
170	34.4	36.5	42.3	46.0
180	35.2	37.2	43.1	47.0
190	35.9	37.9	43.9	47.9
200	36.5	38.6	44.7	48.8

% FAT for SUM OF MEASUREMENTS
AT ALL FOUR LOCATIONS—FEMALE

SUM OF SKINFOLD MEASUREMENTS (mm)	AGE 16–29	AGE 30–39	AGE 40–49	AGE 50+
14	9.4	12.7	15.6	17.0
16	11.2	14.3	17.2	18.6
18	12.7	15.7	18.5	21.1
20	14.1	12.0	19.8	21.4
22	15.4	18.1	20.9	22.6
24	16.5	19.2	22.0	23.7
26	17.6	20.1	22.9	24.8
28	18.6	21.1	33.8	25.7
30	19.5	21.9	24.6	26.6
35	21.6	23.8	27.2	28.6
40	23.4	25.5	28.1	30.3
45	25.0	27.0	29.6	31.9
50	26.5	28.3	30.9	33.2
55	27.8	29.5	32.1	34.6
60	29.1	30.6	33.2	35.7
65	30.2	31.6	34.2	36.7
70	31.2	32.6	35.1	37.7
75	32.2	33.3	36.0	38.4
80	33.1	34.3	36.8	39.5
85	34.0	35.2	38.4	40.4
90	34.8	36.0	39.1	41.1
95	35.6	36.7	39.9	41.9
100	36.3	38.4	40.6	42.6
110	37.7	38.7	41.8	43.9
120	39.0	39.9	43.0	45.1
130	40.2	41.1	44.1	46.2
140	41.3	42.1	45.1	42.3
150	42.3	43.1	46.0	48.2
160	43.2	44.0	46.9	49.1
170	44.6	45.1	47.8	50.0
180	45.0	45.6	48.5	50.8
190	45.8	46.4	49.3	51.6
200	46.6	47.1	50.0	52.3

% BODY FAT from STOMACH MEASUREMENT—MALE

Caliper Value (mm)	AGE 20–29	AGE 30–39	AGE 40–49	AGE 50 +
2	0.5	3.4	4.8	0.1
3	3.7	6.6	8.4	4.9
4	5.9	8.9	11.0	8.3
5	7.7	10.7	13.0	11.0
6	9.1	12.1	14.7	13.2
7	10.3	13.4	16.1	15.1
8	11.1	14.5	17.3	16.8
9	12.4	15.5	18.4	18.3
10	13.2	16.1	19.4	19.6
11	14.0	17.1	20.3	20.8
12	14.7	17.8	21.1	21.9
13	15.4	18.5	21.8	22.9
14	16.0	19.1	22.5	23.9

% BODY FAT from STOMACH MEASUREMENT—FEMALE

Caliper Value (mm)	AGE 20–29	AGE 30–39	AGE 40–49	AGE 50 +
2	10.5	12.2	18.4	20.1
3	14.4	16.0	21.6	23.4
4	17.2	18.2	23.9	25.8
5	19.3	20.9	25.3	27.7
6	21.1	22.6	27.1	29.2
7	22.7	24.1	28.4	30.5
8	24.0	25.5	29.5	31.6
9	25.2	26.6	30.5	32.6
10	26.3	27.7	31.3	33.5
11	27.2	28.6	32.1	34.4
12	28.1	29.5	32.8	35.1
13	28.9	30.3	33.5	35.8
14	29.7	31.0	34.1	36.4

Appendix 2
SAMPLE MENUS FOR
TONY LITTLE'S NUTRITION PLAN

PLAN A
Day 1

GROUPS	# OF EXCH.	CHOICE 1	CHOICE 2	CHOICE 3
Breakfast				
Grains	2	1 bagel	2 oz. cereal, Shredded Wheat	1½ cups cooked cereal, oatmeal
Fruit	1	1 cup strawberries	½ med. banana	1/10 cup raisins
Dairy	1	7 fl. oz. yogurt, low-fat, plain	8 fl. oz. 2% low-fat milk	8 fl. oz. 2% low-fat milk
Lunch				
Protein	1	3 oz. turkey, skinless light meat, cooked	2½ oz. chicken, skinless white meat, cooked	4 oz. haddock, baked
Grains	2	2 slices bread, wheat	1 cup rice, white, cooked	2 dinner rolls
Vegetable	1	1 cup alfalfa sprouts and ½ med. tomato	½ cup broccoli, cooked	6 spears asparagus
Dinner				
Protein	1	1.75 oz. beef, extra lean ground, cooked	½ chicken breast, skinless, cooked	½ cup beans, refried
Grains	2	½ cup spaghetti, cooked, and 1 slice bread, wheat	½ cup spaghetti, cooked, and 1 slice bread, wheat	2 flour tortillas
Vegetable	2	⅓ cup tomato sauce (marinara)	⅓ cup tomato sauce (marinara)	½ med. tomato, 1½ cup romaine lettuce, 1 cup summer squash
Fat	1	2 tsp. diet margarine	2 tsp. diet margarine	1 tbsp. sour cream
Snacks				
Fruit	1	1 med. orange	1 cup watermelon	1 cup grapes
Dairy	1	¾ cup cottage cheese, 1% low-fat	4 fl. oz. yogurt, low-fat, fruit flavored	4½ fl. oz. frozen yogurt, low-fat

PLAN A
Day 2

GROUPS	# OF EXCH.	CHOICE 1	CHOICE 2	CHOICE 3
Breakfast				
Grains	2	1 English muffin, plain	2 pancakes, 4-in. diameter	1 small muffin, blueberry
Fruit	2	8 fl. oz. orange juice	2 tbsp. light (diet) syrup and ⅔ cup blueberries	1 med. banana
Dairy	1	2 oz. cream cheese, light	8 fl. oz. 2% low-fat milk	7 fl. oz. low-fat yogurt, plain
Lunch				
Protein	1	2½ oz. ham, roasted	4 oz. shrimp	3 oz. tuna, canned in water
Grains	2	2 slices bread, wheat	1 cup rice, white	2 slices bread, wheat
Vegetable	2	½ cup minestrone	1 cup broccoli, cooked	½ sweet potato, baked
Dinner				
Protein	1	4½ oz. lobster, steamed	3 oz. whitefish (weighed raw)	½ chicken breast, skinless, cooked
Grains	1	1 dinner roll	⅓ cup rice, brown	1 bun (sandwich/hamburger)
Dairy	1	¼ cup ice cream	4½ fl. oz. frozen yogurt, low-fat	1½ oz. cheddar cheese, reduced fat
Fat	1	1 tsp. butter or margarine	1 tsp. butter or margarine	½ tbsp. sandwich spread
Snacks				
Vegetable	1	6 fl. oz. tomato juice	1½ cups cucumber slices	1 cup cauliflower, raw
Grains	1	4 cups air-popped popcorn	½ piece angel food cake	3 graham crackers

PLAN A
Day 3

GROUPS	# OF EXCH.	CHOICE 1	CHOICE 2	CHOICE 3
Breakfast				
Grains	1	1 cup cereal, Cheerios	1 small bran muffin	½ bagel
Fruit	2	1 med. banana	8 fl. oz. apple juice	2 tsp. jelly (all fruit, no sugar) and 6 fl. oz. orange juice
Dairy	1	8 fl. oz. 2% low-fat milk	4 fl. oz. low-fat yogurt, fruit flavored	¾ cup 1% low-fat cottage cheese
Lunch				
Protein	1	4 oz. chicken, white meat, canned in water	1 egg, poached or boiled	5 oz. scallops
Grains	2	2 slices bread, wheat	1 English muffin, plain	½ cup rice, white, and 1 dinner roll
Vegetable	1	1 carrot stick	6 fl. oz. vegetable-juice cocktail	½ cup broccoli, cooked
Fat	1	½ tbsp. Miracle Whip or sandwich spread	1 tsp. butter or margarine	1 tsp. butter or margarine
Dinner				
Protein	1	3 oz. turkey, skinless light meat, cooked	⅔ cup pinto beans, cooked	½ chicken breast, skinless, cooked
Grains	2	¼ cup stuffing and 1 slice bread, wheat	⅔ cup rice, brown	½ cup spaghetti, cooked, and 1 slice bread, Italian
Vegetable	2	⅕ cup mashed potato	¼ cup corn, white or yellow	⅓ cup tomato sauce (marinara)
Snacks				
Grains	1	5 pieces melba toast	2½ breadsticks	¾ oz. hard pretzels
Dairy	1	⅔ cup ice milk	4½ fl. oz. low-fat frozen yogurt	4 fl. oz. yogurt, low-fat, fruit flavored

PLAN A
Day 4

GROUPS	# OF EXCH.	CHOICE 1	CHOICE 2	CHOICE 3
Breakfast				
Protein	1	1 egg, boiled or poached	7 egg whites	1¼ cups Egg Beaters
Grains	2	2 slices bread, wheat	1 bagel	1 English muffin, plain
Fat	1	1 tsp. butter or margarine	1 tsp. peanut butter	1 tsp. butter or margarine
Lunch				
Grains	2	¼ cup cereal, Grape-Nuts, and 1 slice raisin bread	2 small blueberry muffins	1 bagel
Fruit	1	1 med. peach	1 med. orange	1 cup cantaloupe
Dairy	2	9 fl. oz. low-fat frozen yogurt	8 fl. oz. yogurt, low-fat, fruit flavored	1 cup 2% low-fat cottage cheese
Dinner				
Protein	1	6 oz. sole (weighed raw)	2 oz. turkey, ground, cooked	½ chicken breast, skinless, cooked
Grains	2	⅓ cup rice, brown, and 1 dinner roll	½ cup spaghetti, cooked, and 1 slice bread, wheat	2 slices bread, wheat
Vegetable	2	½ cup peas	⅓ cup tomato sauce (marinara)	1 cup broccoli, cooked
Snacks				
Vegetable	1	1½ cups cucumber slices	1 cup cauliflower, raw	6 fl. oz. vegetable-juice cocktail
Fruit	1	¼ cup fruit sorbet	½ cup honeydew melon	1 frozen juice bar

PLAN B
Day 1

GROUPS	# OF EXCH.	CHOICE 1	CHOICE 2	CHOICE 3
Breakfast				
Grains	2	1 bagel	2 oz. cereal, Shredded Wheat	1½ cups cooked cereal, oatmeal
Fruit	1	1 cup strawberries	½ med. banana	1/10 cup raisins
Dairy	2	7 fl. oz. yogurt, low-fat, plain, and 2 oz. cream cheese, light	8 fl.oz. 2% low-fat milk and 4 oz. low-fat fruit-flavored yogurt	8 fl. oz. 2% low-fat milk and ½ cup 2% low-fat cottage cheese
Lunch				
Protein	1	3 oz. turkey, skinless light meat, cooked	2½ oz. chicken, skinless white meat, cooked	4 oz. haddock, baked
Grains	2	2 slices bread, wheat	1 cup rice, white, cooked	2 dinner rolls
Vegetable	2	3 cups romaine lettuce and ½ carrot and ¾ cup cucumber	1 cup broccoli, cooked	½ sweet potato, baked
Fat	1	2 tbsp. diet French salad dressing	1 tsp. butter or margarine	1 tsp. butter or margarine
Dinner				
Protein	1	1¾ oz. beef, extra-lean ground, cooked	½ chicken breast, skinless, cooked	½ cup beans, refried
Grains	2	½ cup spaghetti, cooked, and 1 slice bread, wheat	½ cup spaghetti, cooked, and 1 slice bread, wheat	2 flour tortillas
Vegetable	3	½ cup tomato sauce (marinara)	½ cup tomato sauce (marinara)	½ med. tomato, 1½ cups romaine lettuce, ¼ cup corn, yellow or white
Snacks				
Fruit	2	2 kiwifruit	2 cups watermelon	2 cups grapes
Grains	2	1 bagel	1½ oz. hard pretzels	6 graham crackers

PLAN B
Day 2

GROUPS	# OF EXCH.	CHOICE 1	CHOICE 2	CHOICE 3
Breakfast				
Protein	1	1 egg, poached or boiled	7 egg whites	1¼ cups Egg Beaters
Grains	2	1 English muffin, plain	2 pancakes, 4-in. diameter	1 small muffin, blueberry
Fruit	2	8 fl. oz. orange juice	2 tbsp. light (diet) syrup and ⅔ cup blueberries	1 med. banana
Fat	1	2 tsp. diet margarine	2 tsp. diet margarine	2 tsp. diet margarine
Lunch				
Grains	3	1 med. banana muffin	6 rice cakes	1½ bagels
Fruit	1	1 med. orange	3 med. apricots	4 tsp. jelly (all fruit, no sugar)
Dairy	1	4½ fl. oz. low-fat frozen yogurt	8 fl. oz. skim milk	4 fl. oz. fruit-flavored yogurt, low-fat
Dinner				
Protein	1	4½ oz. lobster, steamed	3 oz. whitefish (weighed raw)	½ chicken breast, skinless, cooked
Grains	3	1 cup rice, white, and 1 dinner roll	1 cup rice, brown	1 bun (sandwich/hamburger) and ½ cup stuffing
Vegetable	3	1½ cups broccoli, cooked	¾ cup coleslaw	¾ cup minestrone
Snacks				
Vegetable	2	12 fl. oz. tomato juice	2 carrots	2 cups cauliflower, raw
Dairy	1	¾ cup 1% low-fat cottage cheese	⅔ cup ice milk	4 fl. oz. low-fat yogurt, fruit flavored

PLAN B
Day 3

GROUPS	# OF EXCH.	CHOICE 1	CHOICE 2	CHOICE 3
Breakfast				
Grains	3	1½ cups cereal, Cream of Wheat, cooked	1 med. banana muffin	1½ bagels
Dairy	1	8 fl.oz. 2% low-fat milk	4 fl. oz. low-fat yogurt, fruit flavored	¾ cup 1% low-fat cottage cheese
Fat	1	1 tsp. butter or margarine	1 tsp. butter or margarine	2 tsp. diet margarine
Lunch				
Protein	1	4 oz. chicken, white meat, canned in water	1 egg, poached or boiled	5 oz. scallops
Grains	2	2 slices bread, wheat	1 English muffin, plain	½ cup rice, white, and 1 dinner roll
Vegetable	2	2 carrot sticks	12 fl. oz. vegetable-juice cocktail	1 cup broccoli, cooked
Fruit	2	8 fl. oz. apple juice	8 tsp. jelly (all fruit, no sugar)	½ cup fruit sorbet
Dinner				
Protein	1	3 oz. turkey, skinless light meat, cooked	⅔ cup pinto beans, cooked	½ chicken breast, skinless, cooked
Grains	3	½ cup stuffing and 1 slice bread, wheat	1 cup rice, brown	½ cup spaghetti, cooked, and 2 slices bread, Italian
Vegetable	1	1 cup summer squash	1 carrot	⅙ cup tomato sauce (marinara)
Fruit	1	½ cup fruit cocktail, juice pack	⅓ cup plantain, cooked slices	1 cup strawberries
Snacks				
Dairy	1	⅔ cup ice milk	4½ fl. oz. low-fat frozen yogurt	4 fl. oz. yogurt, low-fat, fruit flavored
Vegetable	2	6 fl. oz. carrot juice	2 cups cauliflower, raw	1 cup broccoli

PLAN B
Day 4

GROUPS	# OF EXCH.	CHOICE 1	CHOICE 2	CHOICE 3
Breakfast				
Protein	1	1 egg, boiled or poached	7 egg whites	1¼ cups Egg Beaters
Grains	3	3 slices bread, wheat	1½ bagels	1½ English muffin, plain
Dairy	1	8 fl. oz. 2% low-fat milk	2 oz. cream cheese, light	2 oz. cream cheese, light
Lunch				
Grains	3	¼ cup cereal, Grape-Nuts, and 2 slices raisin bread	1 med. banana muffin	1½ bagels
Fruit	1	1 med. peach	1 med. orange	1 cup cantaloupe
Dairy	1	4.5 fl. oz. low-fat frozen yogurt	4 fl. oz. yogurt, low-fat, fruit flavored	½ cup 2% low-fat cottage cheese
Dinner				
Protein	1	6 oz. sole (weighed raw)	2 oz. turkey, ground, cooked	½ chicken breast, skinless, cooked
Grains	2	⅓ cup rice, brown, and 1 dinner roll	½ cup spaghetti, cooked, and 1 slice bread, wheat	2 slices bread, wheat
Vegetable	2	½ cup peas	⅓ cup tomato sauce (marinara)	1 cup broccoli, cooked
Fat	1	1 tsp. butter or margarine	1 tsp. butter or margarine	1 tsp. butter or margarine
Snacks				
Vegetable	3	¾ cup minestrone	3 cups cauliflower, raw	3 carrots
Fruit	2	½ cup fruit sorbet	1 cup honeydew melon	2 frozen juice bars

PLAN C
Day 1

GROUPS	# OF EXCH.	CHOICE 1	CHOICE 2	CHOICE 3
Breakfast				
Grains	2	1 bagel	2 oz. cereal, Shredded Wheat	1½ cups cooked cereal, oatmeal
Fruit	2	2 cups strawberries	1 med. banana	⅕ cup raisins
Dairy	1	7 fl. oz. yogurt, low-fat, plain	8 fl. oz. 2% low-fat milk	8 fl.oz. 2% low-fat milk
Fat	1	2 tsp. diet margarine	1 tsp. butter or margarine	
Lunch				
Protein	1	3 oz. turkey, skinless light meat, cooked	2½ oz. chicken, skinless white meat, cooked	4 oz. haddock, baked
Grains	3	2 slices bread, wheat, and 2½ breadsticks	1½ cups rice, white, cooked	⅔ cup rice, brown, cooked, and 1 dinner roll
Vegetable	1	1½ cups cucumber slices	½ cup broccoli, cooked	1 cup summer squash
Dairy	1	7 fl. oz. low-fat yogurt, plain	4½ fl. oz. low-fat frozen yogurt	1 oz. cheddar cheese
Dinner				
Protein	1	1¾ oz. beef, extra lean ground, cooked	½ chicken breast, skinless, cooked	½ cup beans, refried
Grains	2	½ cup spaghetti, cooked, and 1 slice bread, wheat	½ cup spaghetti, cooked, and 1 slice bread, wheat	2 flour tortillas
Vegetable	2	⅓ cup tomato sauce (marinara)	⅓ cup tomato sauce (marinara)	½ med. tomato and 1½ cup romaine lettuce and ¼ cup peas
Dairy	1	8 fl. oz. 2% low-fat milk	8 fl. oz. 2% low-fat milk	1½ oz. cheddar cheese, reduced fat
Fat	1	1 tsp. butter or margarine	1 tsp. butter or margarine	1 tbsp. sour cream
Snacks				
Fruit	2	2 kiwifruit	2 cups watermelon	2 cups grapes
Vegetable	2	2 carrots	2 cups pepper, sweet green	½ sweet potato, baked
Grains	2	1 bagel	1½ oz. hard pretzels	3 graham crackers

PLAN C
Day 2

GROUPS	# OF EXCH.	CHOICE 1	CHOICE 2	CHOICE 3
Breakfast				
Protein	1	1 egg, poached or boiled	7 egg whites	1¼ cups Egg Beaters
Grains	1	½ English muffin, plain	1 slice raisin bread	2 slices diet bread
Fruit	2	8 fl. oz. orange juice	1 cup fruit cocktail, juice pack	1 med. banana
Dairy	1	4 fl. oz. low-fat yogurt, fruit flavored	7 fl. oz. low-fat yogurt, plain	8 fl. oz. 2% low-fat milk
Fat	1	2 tsp. diet margarine	1 tsp. butter or margarine	2 tsp. diet margarine
Lunch				
Grains	2	2 small bran muffins	4 rice cakes	1 bagel
Vegetable	1	1 carrot	1½ cups cucumber slices	1 carrot
Fruit	2	1 banana	2 kiwifruit	4 tsp. jelly (all fruit, no sugar) and 1 cup grapes
Dairy	2	9 fl. oz. low-fat frozen yogurt	8 fl. oz. skim milk and 4 fl. oz. low-fat yogurt, fruit flavored	8 fl. oz. fruit-flavored yogurt, low-fat
Dinner				
Protein	1	4½ oz. lobster, steamed	3 oz. whitefish (weighed raw)	½ chicken breast, skinless, cooked
Grains	2	½ cup rice, white, cooked and 1 dinner roll	⅔ cup rice, brown	1 bun (sandwich/hamburger) and ¼ cup stuffing
Vegetable	2	1 cup broccoli, cooked	½ cup coleslaw	½ cup minestrone
Fat	1	1 tsp. butter or margarine	1 tsp. butter or margarine	1 tsp. butter or margarine
Snacks				
Grains	2	1 piece angel food cake	8 cups air-popped popcorn	6 graham crackers
Grains	2	1 bagel	1½ oz. hard pretzels	4 rice cakes
Vegetable	2	12 fl. oz. tomato juice	2 carrots	2 cups cauliflower, raw

PLAN C
Day 3

GROUPS	# OF EXCH.	CHOICE 1	CHOICE 2	CHOICE 3
Breakfast				
Grains	3	1½ cups cereal, Cream of Wheat, cooked	1 med. banana muffin	1½ bagels
Dairy	2	8 fl. oz. 2% low-fat milk and ¾ cup 1% low-fat cottage cheese	8 fl. oz. low-fat yogurt, fruit flavored	1½ cup 1% low-fat cottage cheese
Lunch				
Protein	1	4 oz. chicken, white meat, canned in water	1 egg, poached or boiled	5 oz. scallops
Grains	2	2 slices bread, wheat	1 English muffin, plain	½ cup rice, white, and 1 dinner roll
Fruit	2	1 cup applesauce	8 tsp. jelly (all fruit, no sugar)	½ cup fruit sorbet
Dairy	1	1¼ oz. Swiss cheese, reduced fat	4 oz. low-fat yogurt, fruit flavored	4½ fl. oz. low-fat frozen yogurt
Fat	1	½ tbsp. sandwich spread	2 tsp. diet margarine	1 tsp. butter or margarine
Dinner				
Protein	1	3 oz. turkey, skinless light meat, cooked	⅔ cup pinto beans, cooked	½ chicken breast, skinless, cooked
Grains	2	2 slices bread, wheat	⅔ cup rice, brown, cooked	½ cup spaghetti, cooked, and 1 slice bread, Italian
Vegetable	2	2 cups summer squash	¼ cup corn, yellow or white	⅓ cup tomato sauce (marinara)
Fat	1	1 tsp. mayonnaise	1 tsp. butter or margarine	2 tsp. diet margarine
Snacks				
Grain	2	10 pieces melba toast	2 slices raisin bread	6 graham crackers
Vegetable	3	9 fl. oz. carrot juice	3 cups cauliflower, raw	1½ cups broccoli
Fruit	2	1 med. banana	1 med. pear	2 cups watermelon

PLAN C
Day 4

GROUPS	# OF EXCH.	CHOICE 1	CHOICE 2	CHOICE 3
Breakfast				
Grains	2	2 slices bread, wheat	1 bagel	1 English muffin, plain
Fruit	1	4 tsp. jelly (all fruit, no sugar)	½ cup applesauce	4 tsp. jelly (all fruit, no sugar)
Dairy	2	8 fl. oz. 2% low-fat milk and 4 fl. oz. low-fat yogurt, fruit flavored	2 oz. cream cheese, light, and 8 fl. oz. skim milk	2 oz. cream cheese, light and ¾ cup 1% low-fat cottage cheese
Lunch				
Protein	1	3 oz. tuna, canned in water	7 egg whites	3 oz. tuna, canned in water
Grains	3	2 slices bread, wheat, and 1 small bran muffin	1 med. banana muffin	½ bagel
Vegetable	1	½ med. tomato and 1 cup alfalfa sprouts	1 carrot	3 cups romaine lettuce
Fruit	1	1 med. peach	1 med. orange	1 cup canteloupe
Fat	1	½ tbsp. Miracle Whip or sandwich spread	1 tsp. butter or margarinie	2 tbsp. diet Italian dressing
Dinner				
Protein	1	6 oz. sole (weighed raw)	2 oz. turkey, ground, cooked	½ chicken breast, skinless, cooked
Grains	2	⅓ cup rice, brown, and 1 dinner roll	½ cup spaghetti, cooked, and 1 slice bread, wheat	2 slices bread, wheat
Vegetable	2	½ cup peas	⅓ cup tomato sauce (marinara)	1 cup broccoli, cooked
Dairy	1	⅔ cup ice milk	8 fl. oz. skim milk	4½ fl. oz. low-fat frozen yogurt
Fat	1	1 tsp. butter or margarine	1 tsp. butter or margarine	2 tsp. butter or margarine
Snacks				
Grains	2	2 small blueberry muffins	5 breadsticks	1½ oz. hard pretzels
Fruit	2	½ cup fruit sorbet	1 cup honeydew melon	2 frozen juice bars
Vegetable	3	¾ cup minestrone	3 cups cauliflower, raw	3 carrots

PLAN D
Day 1

GROUPS	# OF EXCH.	CHOICE 1	CHOICE 2	CHOICE 3
Breakfast				
Grains	3	1½ bagels	3 oz. cereal, Shredded Wheat	2¼ cups cooked cereal, oatmeal
Fruit	2	2 cups strawberries	1 med. banana and 4 oz. low-fat fruit-flavored yogurt	⅕ cup raisins
Dairy	2	7 fl. oz. yogurt, low-fat, plain and 2 oz. cream cheese, light	8 fl. oz. 2% low-fat milk	8 fl. oz. 2% low-fat milk and ½ cup 2% low-fat cottage cheese
Lunch				
Protein	1	3 oz. turkey, skinless light meat, cooked	2½ oz. chicken, skinless white meat, cooked	4 oz. haddock, baked
Grains	3	3 slices bread, wheat	1½ cups rice, white, cooked	⅔ cup rice, brown, cooked, and 1 dinner roll
Vegetable	1	1½ cups romaine lettuce and ¾ cup cucumber	½ cup broccoli, cooked	¼ cup minestrone
Fruit	1	1 frozen juice bar	1 cup strawberries	⅛ cup fruit sherbet
Dairy	1	8 fl. oz. skim milk	1 oz. cheddar cheese	8 fl. oz. 2% low-fat milk
Fat	1	2 tbsp. diet French salad dressing	1 tsp. butter or margarine	1 tsp. butter or margarine
Dinner				
Protein	2	3½ oz. beef, extra-lean ground, cooked	1 chicken breast, skinless, cooked	1 cup beans, refried
Grains	3	½ cup spaghetti, cooked, and 2 slices bread, wheat	½ cup spaghetti, cooked, and 2 slices bread, wheat	3 flour tortillas
Vegetable	2	⅓ cup tomato sauce (marinara)	⅓ cup tomato sauce (marinara)	½ med. tomato and 1½ cups romaine lettuce and ½ cup green beans
Fat	1	2 tsp. diet margarine	2 tsp. diet margarine	1 tbsp. sour cream
Snacks				
Fruit	2	2 kiwifruit	2 cups watermelon	2 cups grapes
Vegetable	3	3 carrots	¾ sweet potato, baked	1½ cups broccoli
Grains	2	1 bagel	1½ oz. hard pretzels	6 graham crackers

PLAN D
Day 2

GROUPS	# OF EXCH.	CHOICE 1	CHOICE 2	CHOICE 3
Breakfast				
Grains	2	1 English muffin, plain	2 pancakes, 4-in. diameter	1 small muffin, blueberry
Fruit	3	12 fl. oz. orange juice	4 tbsp. light (diet) syrup and ⅔ cup blueberries	1 med. banana and 1 cup strawberries
Dairy	1	4 fl. oz. low-fat yogurt, fruit flavored	7 fl. oz. low-fat yogurt, plain	¾ cup 1% low-fat cottage cheese
Fat	1	2 tsp. diet margarine	2 tsp. diet margarine	2 tsp. diet margarine
Lunch				
Protein	2	2 eggs, boiled	8 oz. chicken, white meat, canned in water	6 oz. turkey, skinless light meat, cooked
Grains	2	2 small blueberry muffins	2 slices bread, wheat	½ cup stuffing
Vegetable	1	1 carrot	½ med. tomato and 1½ cups romaine lettuce	½ cup broccoli
Fruit	2	2 med. oranges	1 med. pear	½ cup fruit sherbet
Fat	1	1 tsp. butter or margarine	1 tbsp. Miracle Whip or sandwich spread	1 tsp. butter or margarine
Dinner				
Protein	1	4½ oz. lobster, steamed	3 oz. whitefish (weighed raw)	½ chicken breast, skinless, cooked
Grains	3	1 cup rice, white, and 1 dinner roll	1 cup rice, brown	1 bun (sandwich/hamburger) and ½ cup stuffing
Vegetable	2	1 cup broccoli, cooked	½ cup coleslaw	½ cup minestrone
Dairy	2	9 fl. oz. low-fat frozen yogurt	1⅓ cups ice milk	2 oz. cheddar cheese, reduced fat
Snacks				
Grains	2	16 soda crackers	6 graham crackers	1 bagel
Vegetable	3	¾ sweet potato, baked	3 carrots	3 cups cauliflower, raw
Grains	2	2 small blueberry muffins	1 English muffin, plain	4 rice cakes

PLAN D
Day 3

GROUPS	# OF EXCH.	CHOICE 1	CHOICE 2	CHOICE 3
Breakfast				
Protein	1	1 egg, boiled or poached	7 egg whites	1¼ cups Egg Beaters
Grains	3	1½ cups cereal, Cream of Wheat, cooked	1 med. banana muffin	1½ bagels
Fruit	2	8 fl. oz. orange juice	1 cup applesauce	2 med. nectarines
Fat	1	1 tsp. butter or margarine	1 tsp. butter or margarine	2 tsp. diet margarine
Lunch				
Protein	1	4 oz. chicken, white meat, canned in water	1 egg, poached or boiled	5 oz. scallops
Grains	3	3 slices bread, wheat	1½ bagels	1 cup rice, white, cooked, and 1 dinner roll
Vegetable	3	3 carrot sticks	9 fl. oz. carrot juice	1½ cups broccoli, cooked
Dairy	1	8 oz. 2% low-fat milk	4 fl. oz. low-fat yogurt, fruit flavored	4½ fl. oz. low-fat frozen yogurt
Dinner				
Protein	1	3 oz. turkey, skinless light meat, cooked	⅔ cup pinto beans, cooked	½ chicken breast, skinless, cooked
Grains	3	½ cup stuffing and 1 slice bread, wheat	1 cup rice, brown	½ cup spaghetti, cooked, and 2 slices bread, Italian
Vegetables	3	1 cup broccoli and 1 cup cauliflower	3 carrots	½ cup tomato sauce (marinara)
Fat	1	1 tsp. butter or margarine	1 tsp. butter or margarine	2 tsp. diet margarine
Snacks				
Fruit	3	3 oz. mixed fruit, dried	1 med. mango	9 fl. oz. grape juice
Grains	2	1 bagel	8 cups air-popped popcorn	1 piece angel food cake
Dairy	2	9 fl. oz. low-fat frozen yogurt	1 cup 2% low-fat cottage cheese	8 fl. oz. low-fat yogurt, fruit flavored

PLAN D
Day 4

GROUPS	# OF EXCH.	CHOICE 1	CHOICE 2	CHOICE 3
Breakfast				
Grains	3	3 slices bread, wheat	1½ bagels	1½ English muffins, plain
Fruit	1	1 cup strawberries	1 kiwifruit	½ cup honeydew melon
Dairy	2	8 fl. oz. 2% low-fat milk and 7 fl. oz. low-fat yogurt, plain	4 oz. cream cheese, light	4 oz. cream cheese, light
Fat	1	1 tsp. butter or margarine	1 tsp. butter or margarine	1 tsp. butter or margarine
Lunch				
Protein	1	1 egg, boiled	1 egg, boiled	7 egg whites
Grains	3	¼ cup cereal, Grape-Nuts and 2 slices raisin bread	1 med. banana muffin	1½ bagels
Fruit	2	2 med. peaches	2 med. oranges	2 cups cantaloupe
Dairy	1	4½ fl. oz. low-fat frozen yogurt	4 fl. oz. yogurt, low-fat, fruit flavored	½ cup 2% low-fat cottage cheese
Dinner				
Protein	2	8 oz. haddock, baked	4 oz. turkey, ground, cooked	1 chicken breast, skinless, cooked
Grains	3	⅔ cup rice, brown, cooked and 1 dinner roll	1 cup spaghetti, cooked, and 1 slice bread, wheat	3 slices bread, wheat
Vegetable	3	¾ cup peas	½ cup tomato sauce (marinara)	1½ cup broccoli, cooked
Fat	1	1 tsp. butter or margarine	1 tsp. butter or margarine	1 tsp. butter or margarine
Snacks				
Grains	2	1 bagel	1½ oz. hard pretzels	5 breadsticks
Vegetable	3	¾ cup minestrone	3 cups cauliflower, raw	3 carrots
Fruit	2	½ cup fruit sorbet	1 cup honeydew melon	2 frozen juice bars

PLAN E
Day 1

GROUPS	# OF EXCH.	CHOICE 1	CHOICE 2	CHOICE 3
Breakfast				
Protein	1	7 egg whites	1¼ cups Egg Beaters	1 egg, boiled or poached
Grains	4	2 bagels	4 oz. cereal, Shredded Wheat	3 cups cooked cereal, oatmeal
Fruit	2	2 cup strawberries	1 med. banana	⅕ cup raisins
Dairy	1	7 fl. oz. yogurt, low-fat, plain	8 fl. oz. 2% low-fat milk	8 fl. oz. 2% low-fat milk
Fat	1	2 tsp. diet margarine	1 tsp. butter or margarine	1 tsp. butter or margarine
Lunch				
Protein	1	3 oz. turkey, skinless light meat, cooked	2½ oz. chicken, skinless white meat, cooked	4 oz. haddock, baked
Grains	4	2 slices bread, wheat, and 1 cup spaghetti, cooked	1 cup rice, white, cooked, and 2 slices bread, wheat	1 cup rice, brown, cooked, and 1 dinner roll
Vegetable	4	3 cups romaine lettuce and 1½ cups broccoli	2 cups broccoli, cooked	1 cup minestrone
Fat	1	2 tbsp. diet French salad dressing	1 tsp. butter or margarine	1 tsp. butter or margarine
Dinner				
Protein	2	3½ oz. beef, extra lean ground, cooked	1 chicken breast, skinless, cooked	1 cup beans, refried
Grains	4	1 cup spaghetti, cooked and 2 slices bread, wheat	1 cup spaghetti, cooked, and 2 slices bread, wheat	4 flour tortillas
Vegetables	3	½ cup tomato sauce (marinara)	½ cup tomato sauce (marinara)	½ med. tomato and 1½ cups romaine lettuce and 1 cup green beans
Fat	1	2 tsp. diet margarine	2 tsp. diet margarine	1 tbsp. sour cream
Snacks				
Fruit	2	2 kiwifruit	2 cups watermelon	2 cups grapes
Dairy	2	8 fl. oz. low-fat frozen yogurt	1 cup 2% low-fat cottage cheese	16 fl. oz. skim milk
Fruit	2	8 fl. oz. orange juice	2 frozen juice bars	½ cup fruit sorbet

PLAN E
Day 2

GROUPS	# OF EXCH.	CHOICE 1	CHOICE 2	CHOICE 3
Breakfast				
Grains	3	1½ English muffins, plain	3 pancakes, 4-in. diameter	1 med. banana muffin
Fruit	3	12 fl. oz. orange juice	4 tbsp. light (diet) syrup and ⅔ cup blueberries	1 med. banana and 1 cup strawberries
Dairy	2	8 fl. oz. low-fat yogurt, fruit flavored	7 fl. oz. low-fat yogurt, plain and 8 fl. oz. 2% low-fat milk	1½ cup 1% low-fat cottage cheese
Fat	1	2 tsp. diet margarine	2 tsp. diet margarine	2 tsp. diet margarine
Lunch				
Protein	2	2 eggs, boiled	8 oz. chicken, white meat, canned in water	6 oz. turkey, skinless light meat, cooked
Grains	3	1 med. banana muffin	3 slices bread, wheat	¾ cup stuffing
Vegetable	2	2 carrots	½ med. tomato and 1½ cups romaine lettuce and ½ cup broccoli	1 cup broccoli
Dairy	1	4 fl. oz. low-fat yogurt, fruit flavored	4 fl. oz. low-fat yogurt, fruit flavored	8 fl. oz. skim milk
Dinner				
Protein	2	9 oz. lobster, steamed	6 oz. whitefish (weighed raw)	1 chicken breast, skinless, cooked
Grains	3	1 cup rice, white, and 1 dinner roll	1 cup rice, brown	1 bun (sandwich/hamburger) and ½ cup stuffing
Vegetable	2	1 cup broccoli, cooked	½ cup coleslaw	½ cup minestrone
Fat	2	2 tsp. butter or margarine	2 tsp. butter or margarine	2 tsp. mayonnaise
Snacks				
Grains	3	24 soda crackers	9 graham crackers	1½ bagels
Vegetables	3	¾ sweet potato, baked	3 carrots	3 cups cauliflower, raw
Fruit	3	12 fl. oz. grapefruit juice	3 med. peaches	9 fl. oz. cranberry-juice cocktail

PLAN E
Day 3

GROUPS	# OF EXCH.	CHOICE 1	CHOICE 2	CHOICE 3
Breakfast				
Protein	1	1 egg, boiled or poached	7 egg whites	1¼ cups Egg Beaters
Grains	3	1½ cups cereal, Cream of Wheat, cooked	1 med. banana muffin	1½ bagels
Fruit	2	8 fl. oz. orange juice	1 cup applesauce	2 med. nectarines
Dairy	1	4 fl. oz. low-fat yogurt, fruit flavored	8 fl. oz. skim milk	2 oz. cream cheese, light
Fat	2	2 tsp. butter or margarine	2 tsp. butter or margarine	2 tsp. butter or margarine
Lunch				
Protein	1	4 oz. chicken, white meat, canned in water	1 egg, poached or boiled	5 oz. scallops
Grains	3	3 slices bread, wheat	1½ bagels	1 cup rice, white, cooked, and 1 dinner roll
Vegetable	3	3 carrot sticks	9 fl. oz. carrot juice	1½ cups broccoli, cooked
Fruit	2	1 med. apple	1 med. banana	2 cups strawberries
Dairy	1	8 oz. 2% low-fat milk	4 fl. oz. low-fat yogurt, fruit flavored	4½ fl. oz. low-fat frozen yogurt
Dinner				
Protein	2	6 oz. turkey, skinless light meat, cooked	1⅓ cups pinto beans, cooked	1 chicken breast, skinless, cooked
Grains	3	½ cup stuffing and 1 slice bread, wheat	1 cup rice, brown	½ cup spaghetti, cooked, and 2 slices bread, Italian
Vegetable	4	½ potato, baked with skin	4 carrots	⅔ cup tomato sauce (marinara)
Fat	1	1 tsp. butter or margarine	1 tsp. butter or margarine	2 tsp. diet margarine
Snacks				
Fruit	2	2 oz. mixed fruit, dried	20 cherries, sweet, raw	6 fl. oz. grape juice
Grains	3	1½ bagels	2¼ oz. hard pretzels	1½ pieces angel food cake
Dairy	1	4½ fl. oz. low-fat frozen yogurt	½ cup 2% low-fat cottage cheese	4 fl. oz. low-fat yogurt, fruit flavored

PLAN E
Day 4

GROUPS	# OF EXCH.	CHOICE 1	CHOICE 2	CHOICE 3
Breakfast				
Protein	1	1 egg, boiled or poached	7 egg whites	1¼ cups Egg Beaters
Grains	4	4 slices raisin bread	2 bagels	2 English muffins, plain
Fruit	2	2 cups strawberries	2 kiwifruit	1 cup honeydew melon
Dairy	1	8 fl. oz. 2% low-fat milk	2 oz. cream cheese, light	2 oz. cream cheese, light
Lunch				
Protein	2	2 eggs, boiled	2 eggs, boiled	14 egg whites
Grains	4	2 English muffins, plain	1 med. banana muffin and 2 rice cakes	2 bagels
Vegetable	2	2 carrots	2 carrots	2 carrots
Fruit	1	1 med. peach	1 med. orange	1 cup cantaloupe
Fat	1	2 tsp. diet margarine	2 tsp. diet margarine	2 tsp. diet margarine
Dinner				
Protein	1	4 oz. haddock, baked	2 oz. turkey, ground, cooked	½ chicken breast, skinless, cooked
Grains	4	1 cup rice, white, cooked, and 2 slices bread, wheat	1 cup spaghetti, cooked and 2 slices bread, wheat	2 slices bread, wheat, and ½ cup stuffing
Vegetable	3	¾ cup peas	½ cup tomato sauce (marinara)	1½ cup broccoli, cooked
Dairy	1	¼ cup ice cream	8 fl. oz. 2% low-fat milk	1½ oz. cheddar cheese, reduced fat
Fat	2	2 tsp. butter or margarine	2 tsp. butter or margarine	2 tsp. butter or margarine
Snacks				
Dairy	1	8 fl. oz. skim milk	4½ fl. oz. low-fat frozen yogurt	4 fl. oz. low-fat yogurt, fruit flavored
Vegetable	2	½ cup minestrone	2 cups cauliflower, raw	2 carrots
Fruit	3	¾ cup fruit sorbet	1½ cups honeydew melon	3 frozen juice bars

Appendix 3
INFORMATION ON TONY LITTLE'S EXERCISE VIDEOS AND EQUIPMENT

For more information or a free catalog on Tony Little's One-on-One Trainer™ exercise equipment line, Personal Trainer Videos, or nutrition and vitamin programs, please write to the address below. And when you've achieved your goals, use this same address to tell me your own success stories! We have a great award certificate program for photographs and stories.

TECHNIQUE!
Tony Little
7024 Central Avenue
St. Petersburg, FL 33707
813-347-2653